THE
DEE BRESTIN
SERIES

A WOMAN
OF *Love*

D0117620

NE✖GEN®

Building the New Generation of Believers

COOK COMMUNICATIONS MINISTRIES
Colorado Springs, Colorado • Paris, Ontario
KINGSWAY COMMUNICATIONS LTD
Eastbourne, England

The Dee Brestin Series
From Cook Communications Ministries
BOOKS

The Friendships of Women

We Are Sisters

The Friendships of Women Devotional Journal

We Are Sisters Devotional Journal

BIBLE STUDY GUIDES

A WOMAN OF LOVE
Using Our Gift for Intimacy (Ruth)

A WOMAN OF FAITH
Overcoming the World's Influences (Esther)

A WOMAN OF CONFIDENCE
Triumphing over Life's Trials (1 Peter)

A WOMAN OF PURPOSE
Walking with the Savior (Luke)

A WOMAN OF WORSHIP
Praying with Power (10 Psalms with a music CD)

A WOMAN OF HOSPITALITY
Loving the Biblical Approach (Topical)

A WOMAN OF MODERATION
Breaking the Chains of Poor Eating Habits (Topical)

A WOMAN OF CONTENTMENT
Insight into Life's Sorrows (Ecclesiastes)

A WOMAN OF BEAUTY
Becoming More Like Jesus (1, 2, 3 John)

A WOMAN OF WISDOM
God's Practical Advice for Living (Proverbs)

A WOMAN OF HEALTHY RELATIONSHIPS
Sisters, Mothers, Daughters, Friends (Topical)

THE FRIENDSHIPS OF WOMEN BIBLE
STUDY GUIDE correlates with THE FRIEND-
SHIPS OF WOMEN

NexGen® is an imprint of
Cook Communications Ministries, Colorado Springs, CO 80918
Cook Communications, Paris, Ontario
Kingsway Communications, Eastbourne, England

First printing, 2006
Printed in the United States of America
1 2 3 4 5 6 7 8 9 10 Printing/Year 11 10 09 08 07 06

Interior Design: Nancy L. Haskins
Cover Design: Greg Jackson, Thinkpen Design, llc
Cover Photo Credit: 2006 © iStockPhoto

ISBN-10: 0-7814-4450-0
ISBN-13: 978-0-7814-4450-7

Contents

To Jill Wolford-Johnson:

A contemporary Ruth, loved by a contemporary Boaz—

I count myself blessed to be your friend,

for you are, indeed, a woman of love.

How I Thank God For:

My editor, Dorian Coover-Cox:

Dorian teaches Old Testament at Dallas Theological Seminary and has profound discernment, not only into the language, but into the subtle symbolic nuances in Ruth. Dorian poured over this manuscript with love, for truly, she was not working for man, but for the Lord.

The team at Cook Communications Ministries:

They've worked in harmony with their varied and amazing gifts to please the Lord.

My assistant, Gay Tillotson:

Gay's energy, enthusiasm, insight, and administrative skill have made us an Ecclesiastes 4:9–10 team.

My late husband:

He prayed continually for my quickening and supported my ministry, even when he was suffering so with his cancer.

Introduction

I care so much about having deep friendships with other women and peaceful relationships within my family. Because you are a woman, and therefore relational, I know you do, too.

Many have minimized women's friendships, saying they are shallow and catty. I believe God gave us this book of Ruth (Ruth's name means "a woman friend") to stand against that lie, showing the power that can be released through the love and faith of women. Ruth's example comes back to me nearly every day of my life:

• When I get my feelings hurt by a dear friend, I think of how Ruth responded when Naomi hurt her.

• When I want to love my daughters well, I think of how Ruth was restored by Naomi's love.

• When I want to give up because a grieving friend needs so much help, I think of how Ruth did not give up and saw a rich harvest.

• When I feel unloved by God because He allowed my husband to die of cancer, I think of how these young widows felt, and yet how God was their Provider, Protector, and Confidant.

• When I want to guide my daughters in finding a good man who will love them well, I think of how Naomi counseled Ruth in her romance.

• When I want to pray more effectively, I think of the amazing, specific prayers of the women of Bethlehem and how those prayers were answered.

I encourage you to study earnestly so you do not miss the fragrance of this rose. There are layers in the book of Ruth like the rows of petals on a rose, each layer giving a lovely fragrance. Read through it quickly and all you will catch is a pretty, but sealed, rose. But take it slowly, answering the questions thoughtfully, and the rose will unfold, giving you more fragrance and beauty than you ever imagined was waiting.

Special Instructions for Preparation

One of the repeated images in the book of Ruth is that of Ruth filling the empty arms of her mother-in-law. I am praying you will do that for one another in this study by being faithful with the following:

1. Do your homework—every day, same time, same place, to establish a habit. Each day, ask God to speak to you through His Word. Jesus says that "out of the overflow of our hearts" we speak. If you come to the study overflowing with insights from Ruth, you will fill your sisters' hearts.

2. Get a hymnal, because hymns will be suggested to enrich your quiet time. A few are suggested in the Hymns Index, but you will want more.

3. A prayer journal would be an excellent additional tool. Effective prayer warriors take a few minutes each day to jot down their prayers and then highlight or star the answers.

4. In the discussion, be sensitive. The naturally talkative women need to exercise control, and the shy women need to exercise courage to speak up. One reason God used Ruth so mightily was that she knew when to speak and when to be silent.

5. Stay on target in the discussions. These lessons can be discussed in ninety minutes. If you don't have that much time, you have two options:
   A. Divide the lessons and meet for eighteen weeks. Do the same prayer exercise both weeks.
   B. Do the whole lesson but discuss half the questions.

6. Follow the instructions for group prayer at the close of each lesson. Keep confidences in the group. One of the beautiful aspects of the book of Ruth is that the bold prayers offered on behalf of each other are all answered. There is power when we pray together.

One

Love in a Time of Famine

A particular Thanksgiving stands out in my memory. Early that morning my husband and I stood on our back porch in our terry-cloth robes, marveling as the rising sun turned the Nebraska sky crimson and purple. Our arms wrapped around one another's waists, we faced the rising sun and spontaneously sang "For the Beauty of the Earth." Material blessings abounded: a warm home with a fire flickering in the fireplace; turkey, dressing, and fragrant pumpkin pie. My parents and our three adult children had come home, making our circle complete. We cradled our newborn grandson Simeon: pink, perfect, and plump with possibility.

The book of Ruth reminds me of Thanksgiving: ripe with images of the land and the harvest, images of symbolic significance. There is a parallel between the fruitfulness of the land and the fruitfulness of the people of Bethlehem. The pictures are reminiscent of the parables Jesus told: stories of a sower and four kinds of soils, of the vine and the branches, of seeds growing secretly, and of planters and reapers. Likewise, the psalmist compares the godly to a tree planted by rivers of water and the ungodly to the chaff the wind blows away (Ps. 1). Intriguingly, the climax of the book of Ruth occurs at the threshing floor, where the grain was lifted with pitchforks and thrown to the night wind so the chaff could be blown away. Ruth, steadfast and true, is like pure and wholesome grain. She is a woman of love and has so much to teach us. She did not—on her own—become a woman who has gone down in history, and neither can we. But we can become women who love well, and God has given us a book to show us how. This introductory week will help you overview and gain important background information for the rich little book of Ruth.

Prepare Your Heart to Hear

Prepare your heart by singing hymns. You'll find several from which to choose in the Hymns Index.

Memory Work

Begin in earnest your memory work. Over the next three weeks you will memorize the most famous passage in the book of Ruth. You'll do it in the *King James Version* because that passage in that version has become as well known as famous poetry. Begin this week with the opening thought of Ruth 1:16–17:

> *And Ruth said, Intreat me not to leave thee, or to return from following after thee: for whither thou goest, I will go.*

Spend five minutes memorizing today. Often doing a word at a time will help to cement it in your mind. For example,

Ruth

Ruth 1

Ruth 1:16–17

Ruth 1:16–17 Intreat

Ruth 1:16–17 Intreat me

and so forth.

WARMUP

One of the repeated images in the book of Ruth is that of women filling up one another's empty arms. They came to one another offering a sympathizing tear, wise counsel, words of affirmation, or fervent prayers. Sometimes Ruth literally filled Naomi's empty arms with grain and finally, a grandbaby! How have women's friendships, especially those in small group studies, specifically ministered to you, filling your "empty places"? What do you hope to see happen in this group?

DAY I
• •

A Survey of the Land

It's easy to love people when things are going well: when it's summertime and the fruit is on the vine, when your health is good, when your friends are sweet and responsive to you, loving you well.

It's not so easy when times are hard: when it's winter and the cold winds blow, when your health is poor, when your friends don't seem to understand or care, when they fail you just when you need them the most. It certainly is "winter" as the book of Ruth opens. Naomi, the central character in the book of Ruth, has sometimes been called a female Job. She loses everything—her home, her land, her husband, her sons, her dreams. In fact, the book opens with "a famine in the land," a phrase laden with symbolism. But watch, as the book progresses, how the land changes, as do the hearts of God's people as they open to His love and begin, in turn, to love one another.

1. Read the introductory material on the previous pages. Highlight or write down anything you wish to remember.

2. Read through the short book of Ruth. (There are only four chapters.) In each chapter, look for any images of the land and highlight them or write "symbol" in your margin. Also, write a summary paragraph describing what happened in the chapter.

   A. Ruth 1

   B. Ruth 2

   C. Ruth 3

   D. Ruth 4

DAY 2
Everyone Did As He Saw Fit

In order to understand the book of Ruth, we need to understand the dark days in which Ruth lived. Often God will allow "famine" in the lives of His children—not because He doesn't love them, but because He does.

3. What phrase opens the book of Ruth and tells you the time period?

4. Now, turn back one page in your Bible and read the last verse of the book of Judges. How does it describe the people? How did they decide what was right and wrong?

In the university town I live in, there is an ethics professor who is a missionary on campus. Godly, wise, and winsome, he helps his young students think about right and wrong. The first day of class he asks, "How do you decide what is right and what is wrong?"

One after another they say, "Whatever I think is right is right."

The next day the professor comes to class, leans against his desk, and strokes his beard thoughtfully. He says, "I've decided to change the way I grade. It's not going to be according to the guidelines in the syllabus—not according to how well you do on tests and papers. Instead, it's going to be according to what I see fit. What I think. Bribes would be good. I'd like bribes. I also like kids who drive cool cars. These are the things that will determine your grades."

The students' jaws drop, and the room buzzes. *This isn't fair! He can't do this!*

"But," the professor explains, "it's what I think. It's what seems right to me." He's smiling now, thinking, *We'll see how many of them are really secular relativists.*

"What seems right in my eyes" is how the people in the days of Judges decided right and wrong. God's people were no longer "abiding in the vine," no longer looking to Him for guidance, and no longer desiring to please Him. Each had turned to his own way. The longer they persisted living this way, the deeper their depravity became. By the close of the book of Judges, the historical stories are hard to read, and yet, they really happened, serving as a warning to us of the sin that lurks in our hearts and threatens to turn us into beasts if we do not respond to God in true repentance.

5. What contrast to the thinking in the days of Judges do you find in Proverbs 3:5–6?

In the days of the judges, the Israelites repeatedly rebelled against the Lord and fell under the power of an invading nation. Then God would hear their cries. In His mercy He would send a "judge," a "deliverer." The Israelites would be rescued, and a time of peace would follow. During that time of peace, they would again rebel against the Lord, and the cycle would repeat. This happens seven times in the book of Judges, and each time the people sink to deeper depths. In *The Bible Reader's Companion*[1] Larry Richards outlines five steps in each cycle: sin, servitude, supplication, salvation, and silence.

6. Trace this cycle in Judges 3:7–11.

Sin:

Servitude:

Supplication:

Salvation:

Silence:

7. Can you identify with the above cycle personally? Is there a particular temptation to which you repeatedly give in? A bad temper? Gluttony? Sexual immorality? If so, write down how you can see the above pattern in this area and ask God to penetrate this darkness in your life with His light.

Spend a few minutes on your memory verse.

DAY 3
The Downward Cycle

In the book of Judges, God's people don't sink into depravity all at once. True repentance is when we are broken before God and not just sorry about the consequences. Because the people in Judges were simply sorry for the consequences, when the consequences of their sin were relieved, they repeated their sin. Each time we refuse God's light, a callus forms on our heart, and we have an increasingly difficult time hearing Him. Each time we repeat a sin, Satan's chains grow tighter.

8. Read Judges 3:12–30.

    A. Describe how the cycle repeats.

    B. Note whatever you can discover about the prosperity of Moab from the above story. (This will be significant when we turn to Ruth.)

This rather strange story of the assassination of the fat king of Moab by a left-handed deliverer is significant to our study of Ruth in that it graphically pictures some of the material blessings of the Moabites which were lacking among the Israelites. Kenneth R.R. Gros Louis wrote,

> *Eglon, we are told, is a very fat man, a detail which characterizes his sumptuous style of living and which also underlines the plight of the Israelites.*
>
> *... the Moabite king is relaxing "in his cool roof chamber," attended by servants. The one small detail opens up for us the vast differences between the lives of the Moabites and the conquered Israelites—inside versus outside, cool versus hot, fatness versus leanness, palms versus the hills.[2]*

9. Read Judges 19 and describe briefly what happened.

> *... what gradual descents a man may glide from one stage of wickedness to another, under favouring circumstances, he reaches a depth of vileness which at one time would have seemed impossible.... At each successive stage of descent there is less shock to the weakened moral sense.... The sin appears less odious, and the resisting power is less strong.*
>
> *... It is in steady resistance to the first beginnings of sin, and in steadfast cleaving to God, that man's safety lies. It is in the maintenance of religion that the safety of society consists. Without the fear of God man would soon become a devil, and earth would become a hell.[3]*

Though it is hard to believe that people are capable of such depravity, we all are—apart from God. It doesn't happen all at once. It is a gradual downward spiral. Each time we refuse to hear God's still small voice, we take another step lower, another step away from Him.

10. The horrible story above is meant to be a warning. List some things in your nation that would have been shocking a generation ago, but today are accepted.

Spend a few minutes on your memory verse.

Personal Action Assignment

Are there areas where you are keeping God's light out? Pray through Psalm 139:23–24 with your whole heart.

Search me, O God, and know my heart; test me and know my anxious thoughts.
See if there is any offensive way in me, and lead me in the way everlasting.

Be still before Him. Write down what He shows you. Ask Him for grace to make the U-turn, and then do it.

DAY 4
. . . .
A Famine in the Land

Famine was common in the dry lands of the ancient Near East, but God had promised that the land He gave His people would be a land flowing with milk and honey. Yet when the book of Ruth opens, we find a famine in the Promised Land, in Bethlehem, which, ironically, means "house of bread."

11. Read Deuteronomy 11 and answer these questions:

A. With what command does verse 1 open? *Love + Obey FAithfully*

B. What wonders did these people to whom God is writing see that their children did not see, according to verses 2–7?
PAssing on History of God's promise to children ie: opening up Red Sea.

C. Why is it important for us to tell our children about the wonders of God that we have seen that they have not? (See Ps. 78:4–7.)
So they trust in God

D. Describe the Promised Land according to verses 9–12.

E. What promise and what condition for that promise do you find in verses 13–15?
God sending rain
you will eat + be satisfied.

F. What warning do you find in verses 16–17? *We are all tempted. don't take next step.*
Do not worship + serve other Gods. any
Do not be enticed. (morality, Greed, Sin, stealing
Becomes habit + controlling. Don't yield to sin.

Be careful

15

G. How can we steel ourselves against sin when others, even believers, are falling? (See vv. 18–20.) What would this look like in your life?

Commit to obedience
Choose to turn away
Attitude of our heart   *Live by example*

H. What is the promise and the warning found in verses 26–27?

Blessing + Curses

12. Bethlehem was part of the Promised Land. The book of Ruth took place in the days of the book of Judges. Knowing what you know, why you do think there was a famine in the land?

Disobedient to God's commands.

13. The land in the book of Ruth is symbolic of the hearts of God's people. As God's people return to Him, the land comes to life. Skim through the book of Ruth and find pictures of the land or the people coming alive. Watch particularly for images of barrenness or fruitfulness, of harvest, of threshing, and of rest. What do you find?

A. Ruth 1

B. Ruth 2

C. Ruth 3

D. Ruth 4

Sing "For The Beauty of the Earth" from the Hymns Index. Note particularly the last verse, which summarizes so beautifully what God is teaching here. Sing it as a prayer. Then spend a few minutes on your memory verse.

DAY 5

Love in a Time of Famine

Even in the darkest of days, God has always had a people, a remnant, a pearl that gleams in the darkness. Even in the dark book of Judges, there were a few who trusted God. In the book of Ruth, we also see a remnant. Naomi, Ruth, and Boaz gleam "like a beautiful pearl against a jet-black background." God longs for us to gleam like that as well. Philippians 2:14–15 says,

> *Do everything without complaining or arguing, so that you may become blameless and pure, children of God without fault in a crooked and depraved generation, in which you shine like stars in the universe.*

14. Look at the following passages in Ruth. What evidence do you find in these passages that Naomi, Ruth, and Boaz stood apart from their peers, shining as stars amid a "crooked and depraved generation"? (None of these individuals was perfect, and Naomi lost hope after much devastation, but she is the one who modeled love to Ruth initially, and she is the one who is restored by Ruth later.) You will understand these passages better later, but for now, write down everything you see that demonstrates Christ-like character and love.

   A. Ruth 1:16–17

   B. Ruth 2:6–7

   C. Ruth 2:8–9

   D. Ruth 2:11–12

   E. Ruth 2:13

   F. Ruth 2:14–16

   G. Ruth 2:20–22

   H. Ruth 3:1–5

   I. Ruth 3:11–12

   J. Ruth 4:11–12

   K. Ruth 4:14–15

We, like Naomi, Ruth, and Boaz, are called to give love in a time of famine. The famine we are experiencing is like the famine described in Amos: "not a famine of food or a thirst for water, but a famine of hearing the words of the Lord" (8:11).

15. What particularly challenges you personally from the above models in the book of Ruth? Why?

16. What do you think you will remember from this lesson?

Can you say your memory verse by heart?

PRAYER TIME

In the book of Ruth, believers bless one another with prayers. Today, stand in a circle and hold hands. Pray clockwise, having each woman bless the woman on her right with a prayer as simple as "Lord, please bless Cindy" or a more specific prayer, such as "Father, thank You for Cindy's gentle spirit." If you do not want to pray out loud, pray silently, and squeeze the woman's hand to the left of you so she will know it is her turn.

Thank the Lord for MARY's gentle spirit.
(Ellrs).

Two

Distorted Love

Sometimes what seems loving is not. When we love according to what seems right in our own minds, we may actually bring harm rather than good. God's ways are so different from the world's ways that unless we are continually transformed by His Word, we may, without even knowing it, be squeezed into the world's distorted mold of love and bring harm to ourselves and to others.

Prepare Your Heart to Hear

The following beloved Thanksgiving song includes images of the land and of our hearts. Sing "Come, Ye Thankful People, Come" (Henry Alford, 1844) to the Lord and ask Him to grant that you will be pure and wholesome grain, that you will be a woman who loves wisely and bears fruit.

Come, Ye Thankful People

Come, ye thankful people, come,

Raise the song of harvest home:

All is safely gathered in,

Ere the winter storms begin;

God, our Maker, doth provide

For our wants to be supplied:

Come to God's own temple, come,

Raise the song of harvest home,

All the world is God's own field,
Fruit unto His praise to yield;
Wheat and tares together sown,
Unto joy or sorrow grown;
First the blade, and then the ear,
Then the full corn shall appear:
Lord of harvest, grant that we
Wholesome grain and pure may be.

Even so, Lord, quickly come
To Thy final harvest home;
Gather Thou Thy people in,
Free from sorrow, free from sin;
There, forever purified,
In Thy presence to abide:
Come, with all Thine angels, come,
Raise the glorious harvest home.

Memory Work

When Naomi was despondent after the death of her sons, she tried to send her daughters-in-law away, but Ruth set a boundary. She knew it would not help Naomi for her to leave, so, she insisted on staying. Continue by memorizing the rest of Ruth 1:16:

> *And Ruth said, Intreat me not to leave thee, or to return from following after thee: for whither thou goest, I will go; and where thou lodgest, I will lodge: thy people shall be my people, and thy God my God.*

WARMUP

Give an example of distorted love, in which what may seem like love actually brings harm.

DAY 1 ···

True Love Sets Boundaries

In their classic book *Boundaries,* Drs. Henry Cloud and John Townsend explain that Christians often have trouble setting boundaries because they fear limits are not loving. So they enable a rebellious child, a disrespectful neighbor, or an abusive or addicted spouse. But true love seeks the other's good. And sometimes that means setting a boundary, saying, "I love you, and because I love you, I cannot allow you to hurt yourself and me. Therefore

- I cannot allow you, my daughter, to speak disrespectfully to me."

- I cannot live with you, my husband, until you get help and show healing from your alcohol addiction and abusive behavior."

- I cannot continue to counsel you, my friend, or listen to your troubles until I see you are showing the fruit of true repentance."

When we allow bad behavior in ourselves or others simply to escape temporary discomfort, we are not aiding in healing, but rather, as Hebrews 12:13 puts it, we are causing the lame foot to be dislocated instead of healed. It is better to set a boundary to keep bad behavior out and to encourage the person with the lame foot to do something about his lameness. Our love is also distorted when it is not love but lust. Again, we can hold it up to God's measure: Is it helping or hurting? God has set a boundary for sexual expression: within marriage between husband and wife.

1. Find some examples of distorted love based on the following passages:

   A. Samson, one of the corrupt judges of Israel, lusted after a Philistine woman. Read his discussion with his parents in Judges 14:1–3 and explain why this was distorted love.

   B. Describe the "love" Amnon felt for his sister, Tamar, in 2 Samuel 13:1–22. Find all you can to confirm that this love did harm.

   C. In the above story, though David was angry, he did not speak to his son about the wrong he had done. According to Proverbs 13:24 and 19:18, why is a refusal to discipline a child "distorted love"?

2. Are there areas in your life where you are enabling bad behavior in others because you do not want to face discomfort? If so, what are they? How do you think the Lord would have you truly love them?

DAY 2

• •

They Went to Live for a While in Moab

When there is a famine at home, Elimelech takes his family "for a while" to the "country of Moab." The Moabites were associated with sin and corruption, but Moab was not being judged, and the grass was green, for God often lets the children of the world go unreproved in this life. However, God *does* discipline His children. Instead of submitting to God's discipline, Elimelech fled to Moab's greener grass.

There was a famine in the land, but Matthew Henry comments that not everyone left Bethlehem. Survival was possible. Even if Elimelech had mortgaged all his property, as Ruth 4:5 leads us to believe, there were laws concerning helping neighbors in need (Lev. 25:35). This famine probably occurred in the days of Gideon. Food was scarce, but there was food.

Why does the author make a point to tell us that this family was "Ephrathite"? Surely the connection with David is important, for the early readers knew he came from this clan (1 Sam. 17:12), Cyril J. Barber thinks that being an Ephrathite was equivalent to being from a well-established family in Boston, and that Elimelech was fearful of losing his wealth and influence in the community.[1]

Elimelech has often been compared to the prodigal son who journeys to the far country and experiences great sorrow and want. True love sets boundaries, not only for others, but for one's self. Sometimes, to escape discomfort, we jump over the boundary: we eat the whole pint of chocolate Häagen-Dazs, we engage in premarital sex, we skip disciplining our disobedient toddler, or we go to a place we know we should not go, rationalizing that it is just "for a while!" But the enemy has deceived us, for so often the right choice is hard in the beginning, but so much easier later. And the wrong choice is easy in the beginning, but so much harder later.

3. Can you think of a boundary you have jumped because it seemed easier but became so much harder?

4. Read Hebrews 12:4–13 carefully.

    A. Whom does the Lord discipline (vv. 6–8)?

    B. What is the purpose of God's discipline (vv. 9–10)?

    C. When trials come we can choose to stay close to God or to flee. Why is it difficult to stay close to God? Why is it even *more* difficult to flee His discipline (vv. 11–13)?

5. In your own life, think of a path that is pleasing to God but often seems painful to you, and then

A. Explain how going your own way will actually be more painful in the long run.

B. Explain how doing it God's way could lead to "a harvest of righteousness."

Read the story of the prodigal son in Luke 15:11–31.

6. Describe the son's misery in the far country and the joy upon his return. What spiritual principle do you see here?

Helmut Thielicke explains that repentance, though difficult, always brings joy.

Whenever the New Testament speaks of repentance, always the great joy is in the background. It does not say, "Repent or hell will swallow you up," but "Repent, the kingdom of heaven is at hand."[2]

7. Describe the misery of Elimelech's family in the far country by looking at words related to death and despair in Ruth 1.

8. What lies might have Elimelech told himself, believing that his choice was loving? What was the truth, and why?

9. Is there an area of your life where you need to speak truth to your soul? If so, do it now, using God's Word.

Continue memorizing Ruth 1:16.

DAY 3

The Moabites

When a famine came to Bethlehem, Elimelech could look across the Salt Sea to the greener hills of Moab. Although there were times of war between Moab and Israel, basically the Moabites were peaceful. Also, because Israel had become so depraved, this pagan nation didn't seem too different.

Archeologists have discovered that the Israelites and Moabites had much in common, including similar pottery, house styles, social scripts, and languages. The discovery of the Moabite Stone corroborated the incident recorded in 2 Kings that tells how King Mesha "took his firstborn son, who was to succeed him as king, and offered him as a sacrifice on the city wall" (2 Kings 3:27).

Among other gods, the Moabites worshiped Chemosh, and their worship involved sexual immorality. The Moabites would send their daughters to cultivate friendly relations with the Israelites and then entice them to their idolatrous services.

It was to this land that Elimelech took his wife and two sons of marrying age. It was akin to Lot moving his family to Sodom and Gomorrah: a fertile but corrupt land. In order to truly understand the book of Ruth, and the discipline that God allowed for Elimelech and his family, it is important to understand the corruption of the Moabites.

10. Read Genesis 19:30–37 and explain the origin of the Moabites.

11. Read Numbers 25 and describe:

   A. Why did God become angry with the men of Israel (vv. 1–3)?

   B. How did an Israelite show his lack of regard for God (v. 6)?

   C. What did Phinehas do and what was the result (vv. 7–13)?

Sexual acts as part of worship? It seems very strange indeed. But the Moabites believed that when cosmic deities had intercourse, they gave birth to new life in the land, to green hills and lush crops. The worshipers would perform on earth—often on hills in full view of the gods—the acts they wished the gods to imitate in heaven. So the Moabite women lured the Israelite men not only through sexual temptation, but through the hope that their immorality really would help their land produce better crops.[3]

12. God is angry when His children are unfaithful, and He is also angry toward those who tempt them to be unfaithful. What pronouncement did God make concerning the Moabites?

    A. Deuteronomy 23:3

    B. Nehemiah 13:1

Though God had proclaimed no Moabite would be allowed to enter the assembly of the Lord, Ruth not only enters, but becomes an ancestor of Jesus Christ. When we come to God, He covers us with His righteousness, wipes our sins as far as the east is from the west, makes us a new creation, and gives us not only a new lease on life but the power, through His Spirit, to avoid repeating destructive patterns that may have been in our family for generations. That a Moabite woman would be listed in the genealogy of Christ should give us all hope!

13. Have you put your trust in Jesus Christ? If so, share in a sentence how it happened. What are some ways you are aware that He has made you a new creation?

14. What are some generational or family sins you would love to see stop with you because of the cleansing power of Christ?

Continue memorizing Ruth 1:16.

DAY 4

• •

The Sons Married Moabite Women

What should you do if your son or daughter is dating an unbeliever? What if they are dating someone that you know in your heart will bring harm to them? It may seem easier to look the other way, but true love seeks the other's best, speaks the truth, and prays fervently that loved ones might escape the snare of the Devil. True love is willing to risk.

15. Read Ruth 1:1–5.

   A. Has the historical background you have studied so far given you any new thoughts on these verses? If so, what?

   B. Find everything you can about the two sons in this passage.

Read Deuteronomy 7:1–16.

16. In verses 1–4, why does God tell the Israelites not to intermarry with the people of the nations that He would drive out of the Promised Land?

17. What warning do you find in each of the following passages?

   A. 1 Kings 11:1–4

   B. 1 Corinthians 7:28-35

   C. 2 Corinthians 6:14

18. What are some specific things that a mother can do while her children are young to impress this wisdom on their hearts?

19. How have you seen godly parents guide and protect their children from a foolish choice in marriage? How might you?

20. The book of Proverbs has much counsel on how to love wisely. Imagine that your child is headed toward marriage with an unbeliever. Answer the following questions regarding counsel from chapter 27.

    A. What is the contrast in verse 5?

This "hidden" love, though it may be sincere, lacks the moral strength to risk giving a rebuke. Sometimes we so fear losing our children's love that we let them walk into disaster.

    B. How is this thought expressed in another way in verse 6?

    C. What comparison is made in verse 9? ("Hearty" or "earnest" counsel is literally "counsel of the soul.") What does this mean?

    D. What warning is in verse 12? How might this apply to warning someone who is headed toward a dangerous marriage?

    E. What kind of future wife should be avoided according to verses 15–16?

    F. What kind of future husband should be avoided according to verse 22?

Marriage should occur only between people of the opposite sex. (See Lev. 20:13; Rom. 1:24–27.) Believers are to marry believers. Marrying a divorced person is permissible under certain circumstances. Other than those just listed, there are no restrictions; in Christ we have great freedom. Though you may experience less hardship if you marry someone of like background, there is nothing in Scripture that says we are to marry someone of the same race, social class, age, or denomination. If we insist upon that for our child, we are adding to what God has said, and we may actually be working against God's leading. Our commonality is Christ (not skin color, worship style, age, or income). However, there are many warnings in Proverbs about avoiding a contentious woman or an angry man.

21. There are incidents of God's showing His grace to individuals who married unbelievers; the unbeliever placed his or her trust in God after the marriage. Ruth is an example of this. Is this an argument for marrying an unbeliever? Why or why not? (See Rom. 6:15.)

Can you say Ruth 1:16 by heart?

DAY 5

Distorted Love

Most women have a gift for intimacy, and the friendships of women are deeper, more enduring, and more plentiful than the friendships of men. There is a dark side, however. We tend to cling too tightly to people, engaging in "relational idolatry." Instead of allowing Jesus to be our "solid rock," we expect our husbands, our children, and our friends to be what only He can be. Instead of speaking the truth in love to those with whom our souls are knit, we avoid the pain of wounding them, for we do not want to lose their love. Instead of running first to the Lord with our joys and our woes, we pick up our cell phone or send an e-mail, putting another before the One who knows us and loves us best.

22. Why, according to Romans 3:23, should we not be surprised when someone we love lets us down?

23. How do you respond when that happens?

24. What advice do you find in Proverbs 25:17?

25. What reasons do you find in the following verses for going to the Lord first—even before you run to a soulmate?

   A. Psalm 34:4–10

   B. Psalm 103:11–14

C. Psalm 119:73

Personal Action Assignment

Pray through Psalm 5:1–3, and then direct your prayers to Him and wait in expectation for His wisdom.

26. What do you think you will remember from this week's lesson?

Can you say Ruth 1:16 by heart?

PRAYER TIME

In order to love others well, our own love relationship with the Lord must be strong. For without His love flowing through us, we will not be good lovers of others. So often we pray for everything under the sun except our own love relationship with the Lord. Today, the group facilitator will lift up the name of each woman and then give an opportunity for a few women to pray a sentence asking God to deepen her love relationship with Him. It might look something like this:

Facilitator: I lift up Debbie to You, Lord.

Anne: Please give Debbie more love for You.

Isabel: Yes, Lord.

Sophie: Please give Debbie a hunger for Your Word.

Pause

Facilitator: I lift up Sophie to You, Lord.

Isabel: May Sophie grasp how deep and wide is Your love for her.

Debbie: May she run to You throughout the day and sense Your presence.

Anne: I agree, Lord.

Silence

Three

Love is a Choice

Choosing to love people is a breeze when things are going well: when it's spring and the land is brimming with new life, when your friendships are thriving, when you have a loving husband to support you, and when your son brings home your dream daughter-in-law who gives you beautiful grandchildren.

It's not so easy when times are hard. You've been uprooted from The Promised Land and taken to the land of your enemies, a land of immorality, a land where they worship strange gods who ask terrible things of their subjects, such as the sacrifice of babies on the altar. When you arrive, your husband dies! Then your sons want to stay in this land, not just for a while, but for good. They've fallen in love with Moabite girls and soon make them their wives. During the following years, the barrenness of your life continues, for there are no grandbabies born. Your husband is gone, your home is gone, and your arms are empty. Life is as gray as a winter storm cloud.

And yet, even in the worst of times, Naomi chooses to love. Ruth is the heroine of this book, but she had a model in Naomi.

Prepare Your Heart to Hear

Prepare your heart with hymns.

Memory Work

Review Ruth 1:16.

WARMUP

Can you remember a time when you were hard to love, and yet someone loved you anyway? Share what you remember.

DAY 1

· ·

A Female Job

As mentioned previously, Naomi has often been called a female Job. It isn't just that she, like Job, loses so much. It is also that she, like Job, still reveres God. She goes through a temporary time when her faith is shaken—not her faith in God, but her hope for her future on earth. The same is true of Job, but they both come back, refined like gold. Both also experience restoration from God and go down in history as individuals who loved God, not because of what He gave them, but because of who He is.

1. List the disappointments that came to Naomi in the first five verses of Ruth 1.

   lost husband, famine, sons married foreign women.
   sons died, No grandchildren, uprooted twice.

2. Try to put yourself in her place. How do you think you would feel?

   depressed, lost

3. From Job 1:4–8, describe Job's prayer life and his character.

   good faith

4. Describe Naomi's prayer life, even in adversity, according to Ruth 1:8–9.

5. Why did Satan believe that Job loved God? (See Job 1:9–12.) Like Job, Naomi had been wealthy. She had married an Ephrathite. The Midrash, an ancient commentary, explains that "in the old days she was carried on litters by servants, wore cloaks of fine wool, looked hearty, and well fed."[1] When she eventually returns to Bethlehem barefoot and in rags, thin and desperate, the women ask, "Can this be Naomi?" (Ruth 1:19).

6. Find evidences (and, if possible, reasons) for Job's steadfastness from the following verses:

   A. Job 1:21

   B. Job 2:9–10

   C. Job 2:11–13

At first, Job's friends were helpful. Like Ruth did with Naomi, they came alongside their friend and bore his suffering, helping him. Later they misapplied God's truths to Job's life and increased instead of decreased his pain.

    D.   Job 13:1-5

Job, David, Naomi—all suffered and all provide a model of pouring out their hearts to God. How vital that we keep talking to God! We must never retreat from Him, for then we are cutting off our only lifeline.

    E.   Job 13:22

Mike Mason, in his book *The Gospel According to Job*, writes, "With these words, God has just won His wager with Satan…. Remember Satan's taunt? 'Does Job fear God for nothing?' A resounding YES! This man is not just out for himself. YES! There is such a thing as faith that carries absolutely no ulterior motive—in other words, there is such a thing as love! And YES! … Even if God Himself should strike him dead, Job declares that he will not cease to trust Him."[2]

DAY 2

Choosing to Bless

Orpah and Ruth couldn't have been Naomi's dream daughters-in-law; they were Moabitesses who worshiped idols. And yet she has a beautiful relationship with them. She never calls them her daughters-in-law; she calls them benotai, my "daughters." I suspect Ruth Anna Putnam may be correct when she surmises that Naomi accepted Orpah and Ruth because:

> *Her relationships with her sons mattered to her; she knew that those relationships could be maintained and would continue to grow only if they included the new daughters-in-law. So she suppressed whatever misgivings she had. She welcomed Orpah and Ruth, and together they established relationships based on respect and trust.*[3]

Prepare Your Heart to Hear

Prepare your heart by singing hymns.

Memory Work

Before the marriage vows are spoken, if we know our child is making a mistake, we should do everything we can to keep him or her from walking off the cliff. But afterward, we have a different choice. We can lock the door, pull the shades, and turn the light out, saying, "You made your bed, now lie in it"; or we can love that unbeliever, hopefully, right into the kingdom. That's the choice Naomi makes before the bottom completely drops out of her life. We know this because we see the dedication of the daughters-in-law to Naomi. It is most clearly evident in Ruth's vow, which you will finish memorizing this week.

> *And Ruth said, Intreat me not to leave thee, or to return from following after thee: for whither thou goest, I will go; and where thou lodgest, I will lodge: thy people shall be my people, and thy God my God: Where thou diest, will I die, and there will I be buried: the LORD do so to me, and more also, if ought but death part thee and me.*

7. As you read through Ruth 1, what evidence can you find that Naomi's daughters-in-law loved her? Write down everything you can.

8. Read Ruth 1:6–13.

   A. Why does Naomi choose to go back to Bethlehem?

   B. What choice do the daughters-in-law then make in verse 10? What are they giving up? What does this tell you about their feelings for Naomi?

   C. What affirmation can you find for her daughters-in-law in Naomi's prayer in verse 8?

   D. What two prayers does Naomi offer for her daughters-in-law in verses 8–9?

We don't know how Naomi responded to Ruth and Orpah before their marriages, but we do know she blessed them afterward.

Once the decision is made, whether or not she is your dream daughter-in-law, you would *be* wise to bless her. When that future spouse meets you, she is hoping for verbal and nonverbal signs that shout your delight! She wants to be loved. She may come with a lack of confidence, fearing she isn't pretty or smart enough. She may come with the tattered baggage of a divorced family. She longs for you to embrace her, no matter what, and she will always remember how you first received her.

Always, but in the early years particularly, she will long to know that you value her. Be generous with compliments on her cooking, her homemaking, her mothering, and her character. Give her the kind of grace and love you would give a daughter, and she will become your daughter.

A life-changing, classic book is *The Blessing,* by Gary Smalley and John Trent. What is the blessing? It is placing a high value on a person and demonstrating it through words, touch, gifts, and time.

> *Without question, one of the greatest gifts parents can give their child is their blessing when it comes to that child's marriage. When parents withhold the blessing from their children for cheating them out of a "high church" wedding, or for marrying a Greek instead of Czech, a German instead of an Italian, or for choosing to attend First Presbyterian rather than Second Baptist, they hit below the belt.*
>
> *We are not talking about parents who agonize over their believing son who is set on marrying an unbelieving woman or the parents who face the possibility that their never-married daughter may marry a man fresh from his fifth divorce. Yet even in these situations parents can still demonstrate love for their child in spite of disapproving of his or her actions.[4]*

9. What does a mother-in-law stand to gain from being positive and accepting toward her daughter-in-law? What does she stand to lose by being negative?

10. Find all the evidence that you can from Ruth 1 that Naomi loved and blessed her daughters-in-law.

11. If you are married, think back to the efforts you made in the early years as a wife and homemaker. What were some of the specific things you did? What were your feelings (pride, lack of confidence)?

12. What would a blessing have meant to you? What does it mean to you today?

13. If you are a mother-in-law, what are some ways you could bless your daughter-in-law or son-in-law? If you are single, what are some ways you could bless the people, even the "sandpaper people" in your life?

DAY 3

Praying for a "Menuchah"

The word translated "rest" in Ruth 1:9 is from the Hebrew word *menuchah* and implies security, love, comfort, and blessing. A husband is called to protect and provide for his family, to love his wife as Christ loved the church and gave Himself for it. A wife is called to be supportive of her husband, so the home is not a place of strife, but of rest and Christian unity. There are so many warnings in Proverbs about contentious wives, that, clearly, a good wife is one who finds ways to make her home peaceful. A good marriage should provide a haven from the storms of this world—not only for the couple, but for the children and all who come into the shelter of their love. A woman can reduce the anxiety in a home by her own trust in the Lord. When she is centered in Him, her calm soothes the others as well, like a steady mother hen who gathers her frightened chicks under her wings in a storm.

Even if you are single, with Christ as your husband (and He's a perfect husband) your home can be a *menuchah,* providing rest and refreshment to yourself and all who enter. Don't wait until you are married to begin your life. Make your home a haven now! This has to do with the physical as well as the emotional and spiritual aspects. Painting your walls in warm and restful colors, lighting candles, and making sure there is order to soothe the spirit all contribute toward *menuchah.*

14. How does Naomi describe marriage in Ruth 1:9?

15. In what ways have you made your home a *menuchah*, a place of peace and rest, a haven from the storms of this world? I have often been struck by the exhortation in 1 Timothy 2:2 that we live "quiet lives." What a challenge not to be squeezed into this world's mold that involves the family in so many activities, that has the television continually blaring, and where quiet family dinners seem to have all but disappeared!

16. What changes could you make to make your home a *menuchah*?

17. This word *menuchah* is used in Deuteronomy 28:65–67. What, according to this passage, is the lack of "rest" like?

The above description might sound like Naomi was being overly dramatic in her prayers. Yet, in reality, she may not have been. Single women could not own property, and farming was the main way of making a living. Orpah and Ruth had left their fathers' homes when they married Naomi's sons (and perhaps their fathers were not too pleased about their marriages to Israelite men). Samuel Cox said that Naomi feared they would have a life of servitude, neglect, or license [licentiousness]. But a husband could give protection.[5]

God had given the Israelites laws to help widows in their distress (Deut. 24:17, 19, 21; 27:19), but it is clear that those laws were often disregarded, for the prophets railed against the Israelites for their lack of sympathy toward widows (Jer. 7:6; Mal. 3:5).

When Naomi prayed for her daughters-in-law to find rest, or a *menuchah*, she was praying for earthly husbands to protect them and provide for them. Because she then tries to send them both back to Moab, she is obviously thinking of Moabite men. Perhaps Naomi thought that if Ruth and Orpah came with her to Bethlehem, they would remain single, for no good Israelite would marry a Moabite who worshiped a different god.

We don't know what happened to Orpah, but we do know that when she chooses to go back to Moab, she slips out of the pages of Scripture forever. When Ruth commits herself to Naomi's God and to follow her to Bethlehem, God becomes her husband, providing real rest and protection for her. Eventually God gives her a wonderful earthly husband as well, and we see that God answers Naomi's prayer in ways she had not even thought possible.

18. Skip ahead to the blessing and prayer Boaz later gives Ruth in Ruth 2:11–12.

   A. Find at least five things that have been fully reported to Boaz that helped him to know Ruth's sacrificial character. (v. 11)

   B. How does Boaz, in his prayer, describe Ruth's new relationship with the Lord?

   C. How can the Lord, as our "husband," provide a *menuchah*?

   D. What precisely does Boaz pray for Ruth? (The irony here is that Boaz is going to be the answer to his own prayer!)

Continue learning Ruth 1:16–17.

DAY 4

Choosing to Move Out of the Shadow of His Wings

A repeated symbolic picture in the book of Ruth is that of "covering" or "wings." Boaz says Ruth has come under God's wings as a refuge. Later, Naomi tells Ruth to go to Boaz and ask him to "cover" her. Ruth does, saying, "Take your maidservant under your wing." (Here Boaz, as a good husband, is a picture of Christ.) God longs for us to come under the shelter of His wings and to abide there.

When we choose to move out from the shadow of God's wings, we open ourselves to all kinds of pain. Often the consequences ripple out past ourselves to our family and friends, even to the next generation. When Elimelech chose Moab as a place of refuge, when he moved out from the shadow of God's protection in Bethlehem, the consequences were severe, not only for him, but also for his wife and sons. The place that was supposed to become a place of refuge became a place of death.

Naomi seems to be able to cling to God through the loss of her home, the loss of her husband, the loss of her dreams for godly daughters-in-law and precious grandbabies. But when she loses her sons, she despairs, not of God, but of life. Like Job, she seems to wish she had never been born. She doesn't want her friends to call her Naomi (sweet), but asks them instead to call her Mara (bitter). Eventually God restores Naomi, but she suffers so much for a long time.

19. What picture is given in each of the following passages?

    What benefit or what warning is given?

    A. Matthew 23:37—24:1–2

This warning was fulfilled in 70 AD when Jerusalem was destroyed. Historians write that gold melted and flowed between the stones so that the invading armies literally pried one stone from another. The consequences of the refusal of the religious leaders to come under the shelter of God's wings affected not only them, but their followers and generations to come.

    B. Psalm 36:7–9

    C. Psalm 57:1

    D. Psalm 91

The blessings here promised are not for all believers, but for those who live in close fellowship with God. Every child of God looks toward the inner sanctuary and the mercyseat, yet all do not dwell in the most holy place; they run to it at times, and enjoy

*occasional approaches, but they do not habitually reside in the mysterious presence....
No shelter can be imagined at all comparable to the protection of Jehovah's own
shadow...Communion with God is safety.* [6]

20. Each time we choose sin, we move out of His shadow, for He cannot follow us into
    sin. Is there an area of your life where you are choosing sin? How might this affect you
    and those you love?

Can you say Ruth 1:16–17 by heart?

DAY 5

Love is a Choice

There are so many beautiful pictures in the book of Ruth, but one that has impacted me
profoundly is how Naomi chooses to give grace to her Moabite daughters-in-law, and
then, in turn, how Ruth chooses to give grace to her embittered mother-in-law. The love
they choose restores the other and tumbles down to future generations. Philip Yancey,
author of *What's So Amazing about Grace?*, says that grace is amazing because it is not
natural. When someone hurts you, whether it is intentional or not, the natural response
is to withdraw or to hurt back. Grace is supernatural.

21. Read Ruth 1:8–15

    A. How many times does Naomi try to send Ruth back?

    B. Describe the emotion you sense in the girls. What does this tell you?

    C. What arguments does Naomi give for Ruth's not staying with her?

The book of Ruth is filled with symbolism. Here is a picture of moving under the shadow
of God's wings or away. Naomi is in high-tide grief and doesn't even realize what she is
doing by sending the girls back to idol-worshipping Moab. Each girl makes a different
choice.

22. What choice does Orpah make? How do you think this impacts her in the future?

Orpah's name means "stiff-necked" or "double-minded."

23. Why was Orpah's choice a natural response? Why was Ruth's a supernatural one?

24. What choices do you have today? What will you do?

25. What do you think you will remember in particular from this week's lesson?

Review Ruth 1:16–17

PRAYER TIME

A simple way to pray is conversational prayer. Some call it "popcorn" prayer because short prayer "pops" can come from anywhere, and when the "popping" ceases, then it is another person's turn to lift her need. In this prayer time, we encourage you to share a need that is personal rather than for a friend or relative. Lift up a way you long to become more like Jesus or a need that has been heavy on your heart. Also, it saves time to lift your need right in your prayer group rather than explaining it first. Break into groups of three or four.

Four

But Ruth Clung to Her

I t's a passionate scene. There must have been shock on their faces when Naomi told them to go back. We know there were tears. They lifted their voices, crying, "We will go back with you to your people" (Ruth 1:10).

But Naomi is adamant, at least on the surface. The book of Ruth has exquisite poetic refrains. Here there are three iron statements, three heavy chords of despair. But they are followed, if you listen closely, by a faint melody of hope in the form of questions. Murray D. Gowan helps us see the pattern:

But Naomi said,

"Return, my daughters!

Why go with me? Are there still sons in my womb that they might become your husbands?

Return, my daughters, go!

For I am too old to have a husband. For were I to say, 'I have hope,' even were I this night to have a husband, and, further, were I to bear sons, for them would you wait, until they were grown? for them would you refrain from having a husband?

No, my daughters!

For my lot is far more bitter than yours, for gone out against me is the hand of Yahweh."[1]

Prepare Your Heart to Hear

Prepare your heart with hymns.

Memory Work

Begin to memorize a passage you will complete in the next three weeks. This week memorize Ruth 2:10–11. It is filled with symbolism, a symbolism you will more deeply appreciate when it is in your heart.

> *At this, she bowed down with her face to the ground. She exclaimed, "Why have I found such favor in your eyes that you notice me—a foreigner?"*
>
> *Boaz replied, "I've been told all about what you have done for your mother-in-law since the death of your husband—how you left your father and mother and your homeland and came to live with a people you did not know before.*

WARMUP

Think of a painful good-bye you've had to say—to someone who was moving, or dying, or simply leaving the nest. Shakespeare says, "Parting is such sweet sorrow." Why was it painful? Why was it sweet?

DAY 1

Go Back! Go Back! Go Back! (Please Stay.)

Most of us would leave if our mother-in-law told us to go home four times! Orpah is frightened. She doesn't hear any hope in Naomi's words. She hears the cost—she may remain single! Orpah turns back. Henry Moorhouse, in a little book published in 1881, writes that he believes Naomi sent the girls back because she was ashamed that her sons had disobeyed God and married Moabite women. Moorhouse says, "I believe, with all my heart and soul, that Orpah's turning back may be laid at the *feet* of Naomi."[2]

Though Naomi was definitely wrong to send the girls back, I am so empathetic. Since the writing of the original edition of this guide, I lost my fifty-nine-year-old husband to cancer, and I understand Naomi better. It has been sixteen months since I buried Steve, and I am still going through a time of frozenness. I am often not a lot of fun to be around, and a few of my friends have distanced themselves. I want to give the people I love a chance to go away. And yet I am so glad for those who have read between the lines, given me grace, and stayed.

This is how I see the tension between Naomi and Ruth:

> **Go back!**
>
> *I'm not going back, Mother.*
>
> **I have nothing to offer you! Don't you see? I'm empty. No man would want me. Even if he did, my womb is empty. I can't give you sons who could become your husbands.**
>
> *Oh Mother! You aren't empty. Your worth isn't based on your marital status or your ability to bear children. You have everything to offer me. You are so different from all*

the women I knew in Moab. You have a relationship with a God who is alive.

You aren't going to like being around me. Call me Mara! (Bitter

You are hurting—and who wouldn't be? But I'm not going to take this personally. I know that hurt people hurt people. They are like wounded animals who strike at anyone who tries to help them. But I'm not going anywhere. You need me and I need you. I'm going to stand by your side. I'm going to love you. I'm going to restore you to the sweet mother-in-law whom I once knew, who gave me grace, who loved me—even when I didn't share her faith, even when I couldn't give her grandbabies, and even when I wasn't her dream daughter-in-law.

You'll tire of me. You may not get a warm reception in Bethlehem. You may regret this, Ruth, and want to go back.

May the Lord do so to me and more also if anything but death parts you and me. Your people will be my people. Where you are buried, I will be buried.

Well, my God has dealt severely with me! Are you sure you want Him to be your God?

Oh yes. Your God is alive. Your God is real. Your God is holy, just, and merciful. Your God will be my God. You watch, Mother. You'll see. Your God will be faithful, your God will meet us, your God will fill up your empty arms.

1. What comment do you have on the introduction? Put yourself in Naomi's place. Why do you think Naomi wanted to send the girls back?

   embarrassed that her son married Moabite women. Burden to feed, etc. Too much.

2. Why do you think Orpah went back?

   may not have had the same close relationship w/ Naomi.

3. Read Ruth 1:16–17 and list the promises Ruth made to Naomi. Put yourself in Ruth's place. Why do you think Ruth refused to go back?

4. Symbolically, this is a picture of each of us when we come to the crossroads of faith. Following Christ can seem frightening. When people started following Jesus, He warned them to "count the cost." Many then turned back. What symbolism do you see in Ruth 1:11–17? Find everything you can.

Ruth heard the melody Orpah missed, and it made all the difference. Poet Alicia Ostriker imagines Ruth's thoughts:

My heart, that has no proper language, appeared to be giving me wordless instructions. Leave the country of your fathers, go with your mother-in-law Naomi. She is a kind woman and comes of decent people. Let her people be your people and her god your god. You are at a border. Walk across it. You will arrive under the wings of the Lord.

So I went. It was very strange, Naomi complaining, yet I love her. A bitter old woman, yet I cling to her.[3]

God's ways *are* strange. His ways are not our ways. His voice is still and small. It's easy to miss the melody. But it's there.

5. Look again at Ruth 1:11–13 and explain the impossible scenario Naomi paints.

Nehama Aschkenasy writes, "Naomi's language, describing hypothetically the improbable event of her marrying a man that very night and eventually bearing sons, is so outrageously exaggerated that it points to a subtext quite different from the point that is ostensibly being made.... elaborating on the impossible ... paints to hidden desires and hopes.... behind the language of seeming desperation lurks the vision of a potential miracle."[4]

6. What do you think Naomi truly wanted to happen? (Don't be surprised if you don't agree, because Naomi, like most women, was mysterious. But explore her words, exchange your views, and Naomi may come alive for you.)

7. Listening is an art—hearing the still, small voice of God, hearing the meaning beneath the words of our loved ones, drawing out the deep, dark waters of another's soul. What do you learn about the art of listening from the following passages?

   A. 1 Kings 19:11–12

   B. Proverbs 1:5

   C. Proverbs 20:5

8. Eight times in the Gospels and eight times in the book of Revelation the Lord says, "He who has ears, let him hear." What are some ways you might better hear the Lord? What are some ways you might better hear what other people are really saying?

DAY 2

Leaving and Cleaving

The "whither thou goest" passage has immortalized Ruth. Many composers have used it for wedding music. Though the vow was spoken by one woman to another, it is similar to a wedding vow, and the word "clung," or as the King James Version translates it, *"clave"* unto her (Ruth 1:14), is the very same word used to describe marriage four times in Scripture:

> *Therefore shall a man leave his father and his mother, and shall cleave unto his wife: and they shall be one flesh. (Gen. 2:24 KJV)*

In Ruth 2:11 this parallel is augmented when Boaz tells Ruth, "I've been told all about what you have done… how you left your father and mother."

In Walter Trobisch's classic on marriage, *I Married You,* he beautifully explains the three-fold command of leaving, cleaving, and becoming one flesh. The Hebrew word cleaving, Trobisch explains, has the sense of "'to stick to, to paste, to be glued to a person.'… If you try to separate two pieces of paper which are glued together, you tear them both." Trobisch continues:

Cleaving means love, but love of a special kind. It is love which has made a decision and which is no longer a groping and seeking love. Love which cleaves is mature love, love which has decided to remain faithful.[5]

Cleaving. A fascinating concept. There are not many marriages where the couple completely cleaves. There are not many friendships where the two are faithful for life. There are not many believers who have really died to self, left the old way of life completely behind, and clung to God.

But Ruth clung to Naomi. And if Ruth could do it, so can we.

9. How is cleaving described in the following passages? Who are the parties involved?

   A. Ephesians 5:31–32

   B. 1 Samuel 18:1

   C. Joshua 23:8

J. Vernon McGee says, "Ruth was willing to undergo the consequences of following Naomi, whatever they might be. This expression of faith on the part of Ruth was acknowledged of God and rewarded by Him later an hundredfold." [6]

10. Read through the short book of Ruth in one sitting, As you read this time, look for two things: evidence of Ruth's cleaving to Naomi and to Naomi's God, and evidence of God's blessing to Ruth for her faith in doing so.

When I originally wrote *The Friendships of Women*, I was struck by how both Ruth and also Jonathan made promises of unfailing love to a friend. I even suggested praying about doing likewise with a friend. Since that time (and you can read more in the revised edition of *The Friendships of Women*), I have reevaluated that suggestion. As women, especially, we are tempted toward "relational idolatry," expecting a friend to be what only God can be. I found that some women would ask a younger or less confident woman to vow friendship to her, and it was often an unhealthy situation of control and codependency. What I failed to take into account when I saw this "pattern" in Scripture is that both Naomi and David were in extreme distress, and a vow, in that case, was not an attempt to control, but to give support. When a friendship is close, there is an implicit vow, and I think it best to be content with that. Ruth's love for Naomi was healthy because Ruth was cleaving first to God. Then, as God blessed Ruth, the overflow filled Naomi.

Continue memorizing Ruth 2:10–11.

DAY 3

Like Empty Husks

Avivah Zornberg, who teaches Torah classes in Jerusalem, compares these widows—Naomi, Orpah, and Ruth—to empty husks. The walking dead, "Bereft of husbands, bereft of children, bereft of their ability to own property, Naomi keeps telling us, in different ways, that *she* is empty. *She* has empty arms, an empty womb, an empty life. 'Don't call me Naomi,' she tells the women of Bethlehem. 'Why call me Naomi?' (Naomi means 'sweet or pleasant.') 'I went away full, but the Lord has brought me back empty.'"[7]

Jan Titterington, in a penetrating article in *His* magazine, writes,

> *Frequently a woman's feelings of self-worth are strongly tied to success in the "get your man at all costs" game. When we fail to find a lasting romantic relationship we see ourselves as worthless. As Christians we need to be reminded frequently that our value as human beings is something bestowed on us by God regardless of marital status.*

> *… Our hopes for happiness are to be based not on a relationship with the right man, but on Christ and His promise to meet all of our needs, including the need for a husband. Remember Ruth: Like every normal woman she must have desired the esteem, satisfaction and security that accompany marriage and children. Yet she willingly left her familiar homeland, surrendered her rights there and made Naomi's land and people her own. She not only chose to stay with Naomi and dwell in Israel, she embraced the Lord with a faith that might very well shame the children of Israel. And God rewarded that faith.* [8]

I have often reflected on a warning I heard Corrie ten Boom give to not hold anyone or anything too tightly, for we have a loving Father who may pry our fingers away.

Women often cling too tightly to people, expecting them to be what only God can be. When a woman attempts suicide, it is often because of a failed relationship. She feels empty and hopeless because she has put her trust, not in God, but in people.

11. Find four questions that Naomi asks her daughters-in-law in Ruth 1:11–13.

12. Find the images of emptiness in Ruth 1:11–21.

13. What do you think was the source of Naomi's identity? Support your answer with Scripture.

For Naomi, her identity was a husband and sons. Whereas men are prone to find their identity in power and position, women are prone to find their identity in romance and relationship. It may be a husband, children—or it can be in close friends. I have received many letters in response to a chapter in the newly revised *Friendships of Women* titled "Relational Idolatry." Here are excerpts of a letter from Karen of Kansas City:

> *When I read the sentence "… you don't have to be in a homosexual lifestyle to be caught in the bondage of relational idolatry," I felt as if the last piece of a complicated puzzle had finally been put in to place. I had the chills. I had to immediately sit down and read the chapter "Relational Idolatry." As I read the chapter I realized I was guilty of relational idolatry. I was so relieved to know there was a name for what I had experienced, that others had experienced the same thing, and that there were actually reasons why I did what I did…. I never realized that I had been looking to my friend for fulfillment in life instead of looking to God—and that what I was doing was sinful. Wow! God showed up in a big way right in the middle of my family room that afternoon! He became my best friend, my confidant, my biggest supporter, and my most perfect source of comfort (all things that my friends had been to me before this time). And the shame I had been feeling was immediately gone. I always knew something was wrong in these relationships. I knew I was not a homosexual woman, but my relationships felt "wrong," and I didn't know how to fix them. I was idolizing women and not God.*
>
> *My relationships with my friends have changed dramatically. And I don't feel that it required any effort on my part. When I allowed God to be my best friend, my other relationships just changed. He is truly the only one worthy of my worship. He is the only one who can meet each and every one of my needs. (I always knew that in my head, but now I have heart knowledge.) No human can do that, not my friends, not even my husband.*

My friendships are healthy now. I don't need so much from them. And God is answering my prayers for Christian friends. I think He believes that I can be a healthy friend now.

14. Comment on the above testimony. Can you identify in any way? If so, how?

In your personal time with God, sing "The Solid Rock" from the Hymns Index, and make it a prayer for your life.

Continue working on your memory passage.

DAY 4
....

It Is in Dying That We Find Life

Orpah and Ruth take opposite paths, literally and spiritually. Orpah tries to save herself, and Ruth dies to her own desires and puts her trust in Naomi's God.

The most natural response in the world is to try to save yourself. But it is not God's way. He tells us to die to ourselves so that we might live.

15. In Luke 23, other people told Jesus to do the *same* thing (save himself) three times by people in the world. Find it in verses 35, 37, and 39. Why didn't He?

16. In Philippians 2:5–11, we are told to have the same attitude that Jesus did. What was that attitude and how did God bless Him for it?

Notice that Jesus did not "cling to" or "grasp onto" His life. This is similar to the word for *cleave*. Orpah held fast to her old, safe way of life.

17. What similar command are we given in 2 Corinthians 5:15? How do you believe God would have you obey this personally?

18. Remember the parallel God is constantly making between the land, the harvest, and our lives. Jesus makes a crucial parallel in John 12:24–25. What is the picture and what does it mean?

19. How do Ruth and Orpah illustrate the contrast of John 12:24?

20. The person who surrenders her life to God and clings to Him will be filled. The same word cleave that is used to describe Ruth's choice to cling to Naomi and Naomi's God is used to describe the relationship God wants us to have with Him. Describe, on the basis of each of these passages, why we are to cleave or "hold fast" to God rather than the things of this world.

    A. Deuteronomy 10:17–22

    B. Deuteronomy 30:19–20

Can you say your memory passage by heart?

DAY 5

Tested Hearts

In the parable of the sower, Jesus explains how different soils represent different hearts. We often do not know the quality of a soil until time has passed. Some soil may be rocky and thin. Jesus describes that person as one who "hears the word and at once receives it with joy. But since he has no root, he lasts only a short time. When trouble or persecution comes because of the word, he quickly falls away" (Matt. 13:20–21).

Perhaps J. Vernon McGee is right that both Orpah and Ruth, when they married or sometime during the years with Naomi and her sons, had at least taken up some of the traditions and principles of the Jewish faith. But now, their hearts are tested. Are they truly worshipers of the God of Israel, or was it just for the sake of family harmony?

21. Naomi lets Orpah and Ruth know there may be a cost if they come with her to Bethlehem. What might that be?

22. For most adults who choose Christ, there is a cost. For some it is very high. What are some possible costs people have had to consider?

23. Why might a woman who is living with a man or who is married to an unbeliever hesitate to choose Christ? What advice would you give her?

24. How does the way we respond to the cost reveal the quality of our hearts?

25. Using Ruth as an example, how does God respond to the person who counts the cost and chooses to continue to follow Christ?

So often, because of our faithless hearts, we want to know God's will before we surrender. We are not willing to trust as Abraham and Ruth did. They followed God not knowing precisely what lay ahead. They trusted God, not because of what He could give them, but because they believed He was God and would do all things well in His time.

I do not think Ruth came to God because she thought He would give her a husband and a baby, though He eventually did, but because she believed He was God and that she, and the idols of Moab, were not.

Those who come to God for other reasons, as Orpah may have initially, will be found out.

Their hearts, sooner or later, will be tested.

Ruth was able to let go of her old way of life because she had tasted the goodness of the Lord. Scripture doesn't tell us *just* to die to ourselves and to the things of the world, but to live to God. This is a choice when we initially believe, but it is also an ongoing choice we make every moment of every day.

As we seek God with all of our hearts, spending time in His Word, responding to His Spirit, we will taste and see that He is good. We will discover His eyes are upon us and His ears are open to our prayers just as Ruth discovered. We will find that He fills up our empty arms, as He did with Ruth and Naomi. We *will* taste and see that the Lord is good! (See Ps. 34:8.)

26. How might Ruth have tasted God's goodness? (Consider the whole book.)

27. Read Psalm 34, which was written by Ruth's great-grandson, David. Find examples of the Lord's goodness toward the righteous. Give verse references.

28. What are some ways we can die to self and live to God, as listed in Psalm 34:13–14 ?

29. How do you see Ruth doing the above?

30. Give recent examples from your own life of blessings God has bestowed upon you as you have lived for Him.

31. What do you think you will remember from this lesson?

See if you can say your memory passage by heart.

PRAYER TIME

Often we pray for blessings but forget to ask God to empower us to live the kind of lives He blesses. Today, make yourself vulnerable and ask God to help you to die to self and live for Him in a specific way. Then allow one or two sisters to support you audibly. Then another woman should lift up her request. For example,

Lori: Father, help me to cling to You instead of to food.

Nancy: Yes, Lord, I agree.

Kristy: Help Lori taste and see that You are good.

Silence

Kristy: Father, help me to keep my tongue from evil.

Lori: I agree, Lord.

Five

Giving Our In-Laws Grace

I have been on both sides now. When I was twenty, I was the future daughter-in-law, full of insecurity, longing for the blessing. I remember the reserve on the face of my future mother-in-law as I perched nervously on the sofa during our first conversation. She was smiling and pleasant, but I saw fear in her eyes. She was thinking, *Isn't she too young?* (Oh, I was!) *Will she be able to cook?* (Chocolate chip cookies!) *Is she spoiled?* (Yes!) Like Naomi, my future mother-in-law was Jewish. (My husband was a Gentile baby adopted by a Jewish couple.) I, like Ruth, was not Jewish. I was not my mother-in-law's dream for her future daughter-in-law.

Did I give her grace for her initial caution? No! I wanted her to do *cartwheels* around the living room at the prospect of having *me* as a daughter-in-law! Instead, her hands were folded tightly, her voice a bit cool. Instead of giving her a little grace, I harbored resentment for years.

Now I regret that deeply. We lost precious time. When I came to Christ in the second year of my marriage to Steve, I began to give her grace, but even then, it was a trickle instead of a flow. How I wish it had flowed from the very beginning. Philip Yancey says that giving grace is costly. It hurts to forgive someone who has hurt you. That's why we don't want to do it. But Yancey also says, perceptively, that the only thing more costly than giving grace is the alternative.[1] When we refuse to give grace, we quench the Spirit of God, hurting ourselves and those close to us.

Now that I have experienced the other side as well, that of being a mother-in-law, I am much more compassionate. I understand how every ounce of a mother's heart wants to protect her child from disaster. She remembers how young and foolish she was, so she steps up, like a crossing guard at a busy street, and holds out her arms, saying, "Slow down! Look both ways! It's easy to miss things!" (And it is—especially if you are in a hurry!) If her child brings someone home who is from an unhealthy family, the alarms ring. And it is true that as parents we have a responsibility to help our children slow down and think clearly, for many have married in haste and repented in leisure. But while we are doing that, we must also be careful not to crush that potential mate. She's scared. It's not her fault if her parents divorced or her daddy had a drinking problem. She needs you to embrace her. She may not be your dream daughter-in-law, but she needs you to love her and to see, through the eyes of faith, her potential. It really isn't fair to ask if she's pretty enough or Baptist enough or domestic enough. The only fair question is, does she love the Lord with all her heart, soul, and mind? Because if that is true, God will take care of the rest.

Likewise, daughters-in-law need to learn from Ruth and give their mothers-in-law a little grace. Sometimes daughters-in-law expect their mothers-in-law to have it all together, because they cannot imagine that a woman who is so old would be anything less than mature. They forget that she is a person with insecurities as well. She may be wondering if she can bond with you, fearing she will lose her son. So often the daughter-in-law can't seem to give grace! Go all the way to Bethlehem with her like Ruth did? No way!

Even a middle-aged woman can stick her foot in her mouth, and I have! The grace I have received from my daughter-in-law and son-in-law has shamed me, making me wish I had been more gracious to my mother-in-law early on.

Ruth certainly had wisdom beyond her years. If Naomi was less than enthusiastic initially, Ruth forgave her. If the reason Naomi didn't want to take Ruth and Orpah to Bethlehem did indeed have something to do with her shame in their Moabite nationality, Ruth looks right past that. When Naomi is unpleasant and bitter, Ruth doesn't take it personally. She knows Naomi is hurting, and she determines to restore her.

Orpah doesn't give grace and loses everything. Ruth gives grace and is rewarded one hundredfold.

Memory Work

Continue on with the memory passage, adding verse 12 to last week's passage:

> At this, she bowed down with her face to the ground. She exclaimed, "Why have I found such favor in your eyes that you notice me—a foreigner?"

> Boaz replied, "I've been told all about what you have done for your mother-in-law since the death of your husband—how you left your father and mother and your homeland and came to live with a people you did not know before.

> May the LORD repay you for what you have done. May you be richly rewarded by the LORD, the God of Israel, under whose wings you have come to take refuge.

WARMUP

Finish one of these sentences:

As a daughter-in-law, I hope I …

As a mother-in-law, I hope I …

DAY I

Naomi's Honesty in Grief

Naomi's honesty was one of the reasons Ruth understood her. Some have criticized Naomi's negative testimony about God. But if you look closely, she never says God was wrong. She simply says He was severe with her. She grieves honestly. I believe that Naomi's honesty is one reason Ruth's faith, when tested, proved true.

Some people come to Christ because they have heard Christ will give them an abundant life. But then, when trials come, they are surprised! They say, "I thought this road was going to be easy! What's going on here? I'm going back to Moab."   Others, like Ruth, come because they believe God is God and there is no other. Even when the road is hard, they turn to God, because there is no one else to whom they can turn. They have a realistic perspective of the Christian life because someone told them the truth. God is good, but He is also holy and He wants everything! When people were running after Jesus, wanting the good things He could give, He turned around and said, "Estimate the cost" (Luke 14:28).

God hates lies, deceit, and guile. He is pleased when we can be honest with Him and do not try to cover our sin, doubts, and fears. (After all, He knows them anyway.) He is pleased when we can be honest with ourselves through the power of His Holy Spirit. And He doesn't need us to cover for Him to others.

When we are hurting, we can say so, as long as we remember that He is holy, and we must treat Him with the reverence to which He is entitled. I have learned from Naomi. When people ask me now, sixteen months after Steve's death, how I am doing, I don't say, "Fine." Instead, I say something like "I am in pain. I miss Steve all the time, and I still cry a lot. But I am so thankful for the man I had, and also that life is still meaningful, even though it is much harder. I am so thankful that I know God's character is good, even though He allowed this. I appreciate your prayers, and I am asking God to help me sense more of His presence and to trust Him fully."

Our daughter, Sally, is getting her Master's degree in clinical psychology at Wheaton College. One day one of her classmates from the Congo was sharing how his countrymen wail and cry when grieving, but he wondered if that was appropriate, because we are to grieve not as those who have no hope. First Thessalonians 4:13–14 says,

> *Brothers, we do not want you to be ignorant about those who fall asleep, or to grieve like the rest of men, who have no hope. We believe that Jesus died and rose again and so we believe that God will bring with Jesus those who have fallen asleep in him.*

In response, Sally said, "It is healthy to express grief. I think, rather, this verse is meant to remind us that we can think differently about death than an unbeliever. We will grieve because we are separated from our loved one, but we can also have the consolation that our separation is not permanent."

Jesus wept—and so can we.

1. Meditate on Naomi's statements about God in the following verses. What does each teach about God and His character?

    A. Ruth 1:8–9

    B. Ruth 1:13

    C. Ruth 1:20–21

2. Naomi's statements could help someone have the fear of God. What are we told about the value of the fear of God in the following?

    A. Psalm 34:7–14

    B. Psalm 103:11–18

    C. Proverbs 1:7

    D. Luke 12:5

3. If God has dealt severely with you because of sin, why might it be good to be honest about this with others?

4. Are you in pain right now because of sin? If so, articulate your sin and pain here. If you are willing, you can share it at the end of this study during prayer time and ask for support in prayer.

5. Some feel that, for the sake of our witness, when we face tragedy such as the loss of a loved one, we should not grieve. What do you learn about how God would have us face loss from the following passages?

    A. 1 Thessalonians 4:13–15

    B. Romans 12:15

    C. John 11:33

    D. John 16:33

In our sorrow over death, we as Christians are sustained by the hope of the resurrection of the dead. But let us not pretend that death does not hurt, and that grief may not be expressed.... Let Naomi's tears remind us of the importance of not hiding our feelings.... Let Naomi also remind us that our deepest feelings and anxieties are not hidden from God. She deliberately brings her feelings into the open before him, Indeed, she places full responsibility for her plight on God's shoulders!... His has been the hand behind the famine and the deaths first of her husband and then of her sons. Yet she holds these bitter experiences in the setting of his covenant promise, by reminding herself and her daughters-in-law of his covenant name: Yahweh, the Lord. [2]

6. Why might it be hurtful to others to pretend we are not in pain when in fact, we are?

   we may be deceiving them.

7. We may not understand why God does what He does but, according to Psalm 73:25–28, why must we still return to God?

DAY 2

Hurt People Hurt People

A year after my husband died, my eight-year-old grandson, Simeon, was admiring my new silver Honda. He said, "Grandma, I think you should name your car the Silver Bullet."

"I've already named it, Simeon. It's the Grey Goose."

"Why?"

"Because, when the mate of the grey goose dies, she flies on alone for the rest of her life."

Simeon's eyes filled with tears. Putting his small hand on mine he said, "But Grandma, you're not alone. You've got us."

Simeon's precious response reminded me of Ruth's compassionate response to Naomi when Naomi was proclaiming how alone she was. Instead of withdrawing when Naomi is bitter and complaining, Ruth understands that hurt people hurt people. She doesn't take Naomi's words personally, but instead determines to stand by Naomi's side. *You've got me, Naomi,* she seems to be thinking, *and I'm not leaving you.*

> Ruth's response is remarkable, for after she has promised Naomi everything, Naomi wounds her, telling the women of Bethlehem she has come back empty! Award-winning author Gloria Golreich writes,
>
> Her wounds wound Ruth. Naomi is not alone; Ruth is with her. And how can Naomi's heart be empty when Ruth's own heart brims with love for her? But with the wounding comes the balm of forgiveness, Ruth knows (because Naomi has taught her) that in friendship, one must look away, accept small hurts and probe the source of pain. The

source of Naomi's pain is her terrible bereavement, her fear of a solitary and poverty-haunted old age. She has, for the moment, forgotten Ruth, but then she is not infallible. Ruth accepts her as she is, as indeed, Naomi has always accepted Ruth.[3]

Read Ruth 1:16–22 carefully.

8. Instead of throwing her arms around Ruth and saying, "Thank God for a friend like you in my time of need," Naomi is silent. How does Ruth 1:18 say she responds?

9. Why do you think Naomi fails to respond enthusiastically to Ruth's commitment?

10. Now Naomi and Ruth arrive in Bethlehem. Put yourself in Naomi's shoes. What kind of memories do you think came to her mind as she surveyed her home?

When Naomi returns to the land of Judah, she is suddenly flooded with memories: Elimelech, with his easy laugh…. Mahlon and Chilion…. Scenes she thought she had forgotten, vivid with color and feeling, sweep over her…. She is blinded by grief. [4]

11. Why do you think the women of Bethlehem are confused about Naomi's identity?

12. Why do you think Naomi is *eager* to express her pain to this particular audience?

13. Why is it therapeutic to express the pain and the details of a loss?
    Have you experienced this? What do you remember?

14. What happens to the believer who has trouble being honest about her own spiritual struggles to trusted friends and pretends all is well or only asks for prayer for others?

Though it is absolutely true that we should be honest about grief, it is also important to remember that God is holy and sovereign. The following passage is often applied to interpersonal relationships but, in context, actually applies to our relationship with God.

My dear brothers, take note of this: Everyone should be quick to listen, slow to speak and slow to become angry.   (Jas. 1:19)

15. What warning is given in James 1:19–20? How should we apply this passage to ourselves when we are disappointed with what God has allowed?

DAY 3

A Woman of Grace

There are very few fifty-year friendships. Even when God blesses us with a soul mate, we have trouble being true to her for life. Research shows that while many soul mates can pass the tests of distance and stress, they have trouble passing the test of hurt feelings. When we feel betrayed, we withdraw.

One woman said, "A good warm friendship is like a good warm fire. It needs continual stoking." But when we get our feelings hurt, we tend to lay the poker down. And the fire dies.

Ruth is remarkable. She keeps stoking the fire that burned her. Most women would have turned back to Moab, but Ruth is steadfast in her love. She has the kind of faith that keeps her from giving up, even in the face of rejection. She somehow, beneath Naomi's laments, hears the still, small voice of God whispering, "Don't give up. Love the way I have loved you. In due time you will reap a harvest if you do not give up."

16. How did Ruth pass the tests of stress and distance in her friendship with Naomi?

17. List the promises Ruth made to Naomi in Ruth 1:16–17.

18. In light of what she had seen in Naomi's life, comment on verse 17b.

19. Complete the following, realizing there may be repetition and more than one
    principle in each case.

Grace Chart			
	RUTH'S ACTION	GRACE PRINCIPLE	PERSONAL APPLICATION
Ruth 1:22			
Ruth 2:2-3			
Ruth 2:17-18			
Ruth 2:22-23			
Ruth 3:5-6			
Ruth 3:16-17			
Ruth 4:13-17			

20. Is there anyone in your life whom you have not forgiven? How could you follow Ruth's
    model and not only forgive, but give, unfailing love?

Finish memorizing this week's verse.

DAY 4

Grace, Grace, God's Grace

As God has given grace, so should we. Before you complete the following chart, sing a
hymn praising God for His grace.

21. Complete the following, realizing there may be repetition and more than one principle in each case.

Grace Chart			
	GOD'S ACTION	GRACE PRINCIPLE	PERSONAL APPLICATION
John 3:16			
Romans 5:8			
Psalm 145:8			
Jeremiah 29:11			

DAY 5

Mothers-in-Law

Cartoonists, marriage counselors, and even Scripture (see Micah 7:6 and Matt. 10:35) confirm that relationships with mothers-in-law are often troubled. Marriage counselor Walter Trobisch says, "In America and Europe it is usually the mother of the husband who interferes. She just can't believe that this young girl whom he married is able to take care of her precious son. Will she be able to wash his shirts right? Will she know how much salt he likes in his soup?"[5]

Mothers-in-law make mistakes, and daughters-in-law can have trouble seeing them as people who need grace. In an essay titled "I didn't see that you were Naomi," playwright Merle Field shows a depth of compassion as a daughter-in-law:

Wednesday, Thanksgiving weekend, 1971. They are visiting us in our own home for the first time. She walks through the house, past the burlap living-room curtains I have made myself, the bed with a colorful throw which serves as our couch, the bricks-and-board coffee table ... through to the cheerful yellow kitchen with its ruffled yellow curtains. "The landlord couldn't give you a new sink?"

She didn't mean to be unkind. She couldn't see that what I needed was a compliment. She was uncomfortable with compliments. She had been raised to recoil from them…. Once, early on, after an unpleasant exchange, I try to "talk" with her. Honestly. About our feelings. She will have none of it…. Over the years I learned to have a relationship with her on her terms, first cordial, then friendly, then caring, then loving. Loving without touching, a first for me. We built a relationship on the things we shared—our respect for hard work, our frugal natures, our love of things Jewish, our love of her son, our love of my children.[6]

22. In the above essay, how do you see Merle giving her mother-in-law grace?

23. If you are a mother-in-law, how have your sons-in-law or daughters-in-law given you grace?

24. Why do you think this relationship is often fragile?

25. What does a daughter-in-law have to lose by not giving her mother-in-law grace?

26. Review how Ruth gave Naomi grace. Then list ways they were both blessed through this.

27. What do you think you will remember from this week's lesson?

Complete your memory verse.

PRAYER TIME

Pair in twos and pray for someone in your life who needs grace from you. Pray God will give you compassion. Pray for God's richest blessing on her (or him).

Six

The Romance in Ruth

Ruth is a Cinderella story, just as the gospel is a Cinderella story. She was helpless; he was able. She had no standing; he had standing. She needed rescuing; he could rescue. Look for yourself in Ruth and for Jesus in Boaz, and your heart will be warmed. Ruth "happens" in the field of Boaz. Boaz—a godly, virile, and wealthy man—is mesmerized by this lovely young widow. Are there obstacles? Of course! (What great love story is without obstacles?) But is God mighty to overcome those obstacles? You know He is, especially for those who fear Him, who have come "under the shadow of His wings."

Prepare Your Heart to Hear

Prepare your heart with a "harvest" hymn.

Memory Work

Finish memorizing Ruth 2:10–13, adding verse 13.

At this, she bowed down with her face to the ground. She exclaimed, "Why have I found such favor in your eyes that you notice me—a foreigner?"
Boaz replied, "I've been told all about what you have done for your mother-in-law since the death of your husband—how you left your father and mother and your homeland and came to live with a people you did not know before. May the LORD repay you for what you have done. May you be richly rewarded by the LORD, the God of Israel, under whose wings you have come to take refuge."
"May I continue to find favor in your eyes, my lord," she said. "You have given me comfort and have spoken kindly to your servant—though I do not have the standing of one of your servant girls."

WARMUP

In one breath, have a few tell about one of their favorite love stories (book, movie, personal).

DAY 1

The Barley Harvest Was Beginning

The first chapter of Ruth, a chapter of famine and death, closes with a melody of hope. Two widows arrive "in Bethlehem as the barley harvest was beginning" (1:22). God is providing for His people again, and the fields are full of hundreds of enthusiastic reapers and gleaners. Samuel Cox paints the scene:

> *The field is thick with waving barley. The reapers cut their way into it with sickles…. Behind them the women gather up the armfuls and bind them into sheaves. Still further in the rear follow the widow and stranger, who, according to the Hebrew law, have the right to glean after the reapers…. (Skins filled with water hang from the branch of a nearby tree, kept cool by the soft breeze. A house is also there in which those who are weary may rest from the glare and heat of the sun.)[1]*

1. What contrast do you see in the land between the opening of chapter 1 and the end? What significance?

2. Ruth 2:1 gives us a clue as to the identity of the agent of redemption. Who is he, and what do you learn about him?

3. When we are told Boaz is from the clan of Elimelech, the faint melody of Ruth 1 grows stronger. When you were from the same clan, you were considered "a brother." What do we learn about a brother's responsibility in Deuteronomy 25:5–10?

4. In Ruth 2:2, Ruth shows knowledge of another levitical law found in Deuteronomy 24:19–22. What was it?

5. What reason does God give in Deuteronomy 24:19 for being kind to the less fortunate?

6. What reason does He give in Deuteronomy 24:22 for being kind? What do you think He means by this?

7. Scripture often tells us that we are to love others as we have been loved by God. Explain how you see this in the following passages:

   A. 2 Corinthians 5:18–20

   B. Ephesians 5:29–32

   C. 1 John 3:16–17

8. We become more compassionate when we remember what it was like to be hurting. God wants the Israelites to remember their years in slavery and as strangers in a foreign land. If possible, recall your pain when you were

   A. Going through adolescence

   B. In darkness, in slavery to sin

   C. New in town

9. What does 2 Corinthians 1:3–4 teach?

10. Through what kinds of troubles has God brought you so that you are now equipped to bring comfort to others?

11. Is God speaking to you in some way to be more compassionate to someone who is in one of the above situations? If so, what action will you take?

DAY 2

There Was a Relative of Naomi's Husband

I have a dear friend whose story parallels Ruth's in many ways. Knowing and loving Jill has brought the story of Ruth alive for me in a contemporary setting. I first met Jill more than twenty years ago when she and her husband Russ were at a track meet. The picture vivid in my memory is of Russ Wolford that day. A big, handsome farmer, Russ had four-year-old Geri perched high upon his shoulders as he led the family in cheers for Gina who was leading in the one-hundred-yard dash. The five on the sidelines screamed and whooped, and then embraced in a jubilant heap when Gina was first over the finish line. All who watched this loving family were warmed.

No one expected that tragedy lurked around the corner. A year later Russ Wolford was electrocuted in a farming accident. I visited Jill out at the Wolford farm in her dark days of grief. She was too thin, and her smile, though brave, quivered. She told me she wanted to hold on to the farm for the children's sake, but how? She said the children weren't sleeping: they had nightmares about the accident, of their dad's still body. I wept with her. Together we prayed to God, under whose wings she and the children had taken refuge.

Jill played a song for me that the children had been listening to over and over again on their little tape recorder. *Cover Me* by Andrew Culverwell calmed the children with images of security and protection, taken from word pictures in Ruth (Lyrics on page 119). It seemed to be the only thing that helped them fall asleep.

Unable to operate the farm, Jill reluctantly rented it out and moved the family to town. But, like Ruth, she trusted God. Still young, still beautiful, Jill was cautious when men began to inquire concerning her availability. She wanted only God's choice. Years passed.

I stopped to visit Jill one Christmas and she was radiant. With a shy smile, she said, "Dee, I've met someone."

"Tell me everything!" (I was sounding like Naomi in Ruth 3:16.) And with detail that cannot fit in a Bible study guide, she told me all about Keith Johnson, a godly man, a farmer, who had been through his own personal grief, but was now obviously winning her heart.

I remember their wedding day, a scene reminiscent of the wedding day of Ruth and Boaz. The people of God, who loved them so, rejoiced that the time of sadness was over! We knew challenges lay ahead, but we had seen God's hand in their romance, and now we prayed in faith, much as the people of Bethlehem prayed for Ruth and Boaz on their wedding day. Jill, Keith, and the four children stood in a circle at the front of the church, arms intertwined, heads bowed, as the body of Christ prayed for their new family.

Boaz bought back the farm that belonged to Ruth's late husband, brother-in-law, and father-in-law. He raised up their first son in the late family's name. He embraced Naomi as part of the family. It takes a godly man to do those things.

Keith sold his own property in order to redeem Jill's rented farm and to purchase additional adjoining acreage that belonged to Jill's brother-in-law, Roger Wolford. The family moved back to their farm where Keith erected a sign: "The Wolford-Johnsons." The Wolford name has not been blotted out. In addition, Keith has embraced the extended family. As Boaz brought Naomi into his home, Keith has kept the children in close contact with Russ's parents. It takes a godly man to do those things.

Every time I drive by the Wolford-Johnsons, I think of Ruth and Boaz, and of our God, who is eager to give refuge to those of noble character, and who sees to it that the name of the righteous is not blotted out. I wrote this original guide ten years ago, and now I have a wonderful update. Keith and Jill raised those four little children in the nurture and admonition of the Lord, and today they all are married adults, serving the Lord wholeheartedly. Recording artist and co-author of our curriculum *Falling In Love with Jesus*, Kathy Troccoli told me, "I've met a lot of Bozos, but I've never met a Boaz. I want to meet this Boaz." So when Kathy visited me in Nebraska, we went to dinner at Keith and Jill's. Keith took Kathy for a ride on a combine (she kept calling it a concubine), and she was struck by how vibrant Jesus was in this couple. (It is to this Jill that I have dedicated this guide.)

G. Campbell Morgan says that the lives of Ruth and Boaz illustrate "saintship." Ruth trusted God amid desperate circumstances. She and Boaz lived godly lives in the degenerate days of the judges. Morgan describes the character of each:

> *Ruth was a woman capable of love, characterized by modesty, of fine gentleness, of splendid courage; a woman in all the grace and beauty of womanhood. Boaz was a man of integrity, of courtesy, of tender passion, of courage; a man in all the strength and glory of manhood.*[2]

Bible study methods are intended to help you slow down and see more. One method that is particularly helpful is structuring. In structuring a passage you

• Write down every word in order;

• Look for complete independent phrases and put them on the far left of your paper in darker letters or caps;

• Indent incomplete dependent phrases and put them above or below the word to which they link, to which they are dependent upon.

For example, this is how I would structure Ruth 1:1 (NKJV):

NOW IT CAME TO PASS

     IN THE DAYS

          WHEN THE JUDGES RULED THAT

THERE WAS A FAMINE IN THE LAND

     AND

A CERTAIN MAN OF BETHLEHEM, JUDAH, WENT TO DWELL IN THE COUNTRY OF MOAB

    HE

     AND

      HIS WIFE
     AND

      HIS TWO SONS.

Structuring helps you see things. By doing the above verse, here are just a few of the things I discovered:

• The story begins by framing the time—it took place in the days of Judges. So, I can ask, why is this important? (Because in those days every man did what was right in his own eyes.)

• The first complete phrase was "There was a famine in the land." Why does God have this stand out? (Because the land is pictured throughout Ruth symbolically.)

• The man's choice had a domino effect on his wife and two sons.

12. Now, you try it with Ruth 2:1–2. Do it yourself, before you look at how I did it in the Leader's Notes. Do the best you can and then see what you discover. Look again at the guidelines for structuring above. Even if you don't do it exactly right, you'll see things you didn't see before. (Use the next page to structure Ruth 2:1 and the page following for Ruth 2:2.)

Ruth 2:1

Ruth 2:2

13. What questions or reflections come to mind concerning Ruth 2:1–2 because of the above exercise? Discuss them in your group.

DAY 3
● ●

Boaz—an Earthly Bridegroom Reflecting Christ

Godly men are incredibly attractive. There is a richness, a depth, a warmth and a sensitivity in godly men that dwarfs the spiritually anemic. Boaz was such a man! Robert A. Watson says, "From the moment he appears in the narrative, we note in him a certain largeness of character."[3]

Some have thought that Boaz was an old man because of his words in Ruth 3:10 when he blesses Ruth for not running after the younger men. But this doesn't mean that Boaz was old. J. Vernon McGee says, "The normal inference from this passage is that Boaz was not a boy but a man of middle age. Quite evidently, he was in the full vigor of manhood...."[4] Yet certainly one of the obstacles in this romance is that both Ruth and Boaz regarded the other as somewhat unattainable. He sees a lovely young woman who probably would want a younger man. She sees a "man of standing" who probably wouldn't want a destitute Moabitess. It reminds me of the conflict in the movie *South Pacific* when he is an older cultured Frenchman, and she is a "little hick from Little Rock." In their song, "We Are Not Alike," they cannot imagine the other would be attainable.

But, of course, when God is in it, obstacles can be overcome, and, they are. Both poverty and wealth test character. Boaz passed the test of wealth. He ate with his servants, he remembered the poor, and he was ever mindful of the Lord.

What a guy!

Read Ruth 2:3–5.

14. As Ruth goes out and chooses from all the fields in Bethlehem, in whose field does she "happen"?

15. What fact does the author of Ruth repeat about Boaz in verse 3? Why do you think this fact is repeated?

16. Describe the kind of man that Boaz seems to be in our first glimpse of him in verse 4.

There is no separation between the sacred and the secular; the whole of life is lived as "before the face of God." Here we have what Alexander Maclaren calls the "lovely little picture of a harvest field, where passers-by shout their good wishes to the glad toilers, and are answered by these with like salutations. 'The blessing of the Lord be upon you! We bless you in the name of the Lord.'"[5]

17. How might verse 5 demonstrate an immediate answer to prayer?

18. What are the prayers called out in verse 4?

19. What does Boaz's question reveal about the culture?

20. Read Ruth 2:6–9.

   A. What does Boaz learn about Ruth's character from his foreman?

   B. Look at each sentence Boaz speaks to Ruth in 2:8–9 and explain how he understood and met her fears and needs.

   C. Boaz's greeting demonstrates a robust and thankful spirit. Thankful spirits are often generous. Why do you think that is?

21. What are your impressions of Boaz at this point? Why?

Hidden in every book in the Old Testament is Jesus, for the Old Testament is the drumbeat for the entrance of Christ in the New Testament. In the book of Ruth, Christ is hidden in the figure of Boaz. This will become increasingly clear in Ruth 3, when Boaz becomes the "kinsman-redeemer."

22. How can you see Christ in the figure of Boaz in Ruth 2:8–9?

23. How has Christ provided for you or protected you recently?

24. How does Ruth respond to Boaz in Ruth 2:10?

Read 2 Samuel 9.

There is a beautiful parallel here. Ruth's great-grandson, David, treats the crippled Mephibosheth with kindness that resembles that of Boaz toward Ruth. In biblical days, disabled people were not valued. Also, family members of the previous king were often executed, so there would be no threat to the new king. This helps us to understand why Mephibosheth, when called before the king, is so afraid.

25. Compare Ruth 2:8–10 and 2 Samuel 9. Find similarities in the attitude, posture, and words of Ruth and Mephibosheth.

26. Look briefly ahead to Ruth 3:11 and compare it to 2 Samuel 9:7. What similarity do you see?

27. Compare both of these scenes to the scene in Isaiah 6:1–7 in which Isaiah saw the Lord. What similarities do you see?

28. When you see the Lord face-to-face, how do you think you will feel? What do you think He will say to you?

Review your memory work.

DAY 4
. . . .

Love Is a Many-Splendored Thing

What makes romance *especially* exciting? The hand of God! Surely the author of Ruth wants us to know that this is not a chance meeting. Out of all the fields of Bethlehem, "as it turned out," Ruth finds herself in the field of Boaz. And "just then" Boaz arrives. He notices her and tells her why.

29. Read Ruth 2:10–17.

A. What has impressed Boaz about Ruth?

B. How does he show her that he understands the difficulty of what she has done?

C. How does he pray for her?

Some have said Boaz is shirking his responsibility here. (Jas. 2:15–16 says if we are equipped to help, we shouldn't just pray that God will help the destitute.) However, Boaz does help Ruth, although he does not propose marriage according to the Mosaic Law.

Perhaps he is unsure of her interest. Perhaps he is aware of the nearer kinsman who should be given the first right to propose.

30. The word picture that Boaz gives is a theme in Scripture. What else do you learn about the character of God from:

    A. Psalm 17:8

    B. Psalm 36:7

    C. Psalm 57:1

    D. Psalm 63:7

31. How does Boaz continue to show kindness to Ruth in 2:14?

32. Based on this account, what advice would you give to a woman who hopes to attract a godly man?

Can you say both memory passages from Ruth by heart?

DAY 5

. . . .

My God Has Not Forgotten Me!

It's a heartwarming scene. Ruth has been determined to fill the empty arms of her mother-in-law. Now she comes home carrying a huge bag of freshly threshed grain. Naomi, amazed, asks who has been so kind to Ruth. Cyril Barber says that "the innocent way in which Ruth mentions Boaz's name shows she has no idea of the dramatic import of her words." [6]

It is the climax of the book. How interesting that Ruth is bringing home arms full of harvested grain. It is a picture full of symbolism—and not lost on Naomi. Her heart is restored as she cries, "My God has not forgotten me!"

33. Read Ruth 2:17–23.

    A. Describe Ruth's work habits (vv. 17–18).

The grain was so plentiful, Ruth had to thresh it. Even threshed, it amounted to three-fifths of a bushel.

    B. Describe Ruth's eating habits (v. 18).

In studying thin people, I learned that they do four fundamental things that fat people don't. They hardly ever eat unless their body is hungry. They eat exactly what they want to eat. They don't eat unconsciously: they stay conscious of what they are eating and the effect it's having on their body. They stop eating when their body's hunger goes away.[7]

34. Notice the escalating excitement between Naomi and Ruth.

    A. How can you see initial excitement in Naomi in verse 19?

    B. How does Ruth's innocent reply escalate Naomi's excitement (vv. 19–20)?

    C. How does Ruth now add to the excitement (v. 21)?

    D. How does Naomi change from apathy to action (v. 22)?

    E. What symbolism do you see in the similar warning of both Boaz and Naomi to Ruth in 2:8–9 and 2:22? How might this apply to us spiritually?

    F. What picture of the land is given at the close of chapter 2? Since pictures of the land are significant in Ruth, what hope does this give?

35. Like gently moving streams, Ruth and Naomi join together, giving one another a fresh water supply and the energy to enter the rushing, exciting river of God. Think about a time when you and a sister (or sisters) in Christ helped each other ride the exciting rapids of God's will. Share. (And in the sharing, you will be escalating the group's excitement in the wonder of being children of God.)

36. Ruth provides a model for restoring the brokenhearted. The following verses give advice on this subject. Explain first what they tell us to do (or not to do) if we are going to restore another. Then explain how Ruth did it right!

   A. Proverbs 20:6

   B. Proverbs 25:20

   C. Romans 12:12–14

   D. Galatians 6:9–10

   E. 1 Peter 4:8

37. What has God impressed on your heart from this entire lesson?

PRAYER TIME

In conversational prayer, lift up your own need (or an impression described in question 37) and allow two or three other women to say sentence prayers for you. When there is a pause, another woman should lift up her need. Close with "God Is So Good" or another familiar chorus.

Seven

Matchmaker, Matchmaker

Naomi, numbed by grief, has awakened. Ruth, through her steadfast kindnesses and faith, has brought restoration to Naomi.

Now Naomi is going to see to the redeeming of Ruth.

How good of God to give us this beautiful portrait of the power, the value, and the sheer beauty of women's friendships.

All my life, women have ministered to me through friendship. Women are like roses: breathtakingly beautiful, created to open petal after petal of fragrant loveliness in a world often devoid of softness and beauty. Yes, we have thorns, but the beauty of the rose more than compensates for the occasional jab of a thorn.

After one conference where I spoke about women's friendships, a woman stood during the sharing time and said,

> We're always being told that women are catty, gossipy, and shallow. It was so good to hear about the beauty of women's friendships. It strikes a true chord in my heart, one I have needed to hear. As sisters in Christ, we and our friendships have worth in God's eyes.

I am absolutely convinced that God gave us the book of Ruth, in part, to affirm us as women, to remind us of our value and of our value to one another.

Memory Work

Memorize Ruth 3:9, a key verse, this week.

> "Who are you?" he asked.
> "I am your servant Ruth," she said. "Spread the corner of your garment over me, since you are a kinsman-redeemer."

WARMUP

Go around the circle clockwise, having each woman share one reason she is thankful for the woman on her right.

DAY 1 ....

Mara has Left and Naomi is Back!

Some friends infuse our faith, some friends share our faith, and some friends sap our faith. Ruth has definitely infused Naomi's lagging faith. Ruth has taken enormous risks, and God has met her at each turn. Naomi has watched, and now Naomi's faith in the goodness of God has been restored and her hope for the future is rekindled. Depression and discouragement are gone. Mara has left and Naomi is back! As Naomi flies into action with a deliberate matchmaking plan, we begin to understand why her daughter-in-law was so devoted to her. She makes me smile. As you read Ruth 3, see how active Naomi is in helping Ruth, how respectful Ruth is of Naomi, and how intimately they share. This is friendship at its best.

Naomi came up with a bold plan. And despite the seeming audacity of it, despite the risk of danger or embarrassment, Ruth follows Naomi's plan to the letter. She trusts this woman, and she trusts this woman's God.

After oxen had tramped out the grain, men threw it into the air with a pitchfork against the night wind. The chaff would be blown away and the good grain would fall to the ground. It was the climax of the harvest and had the spirit of a religious festival. Families enjoyed bonfires, food, and festivity. Ruth could be lost in the crowd. After the people went home, a few men slept there to guard the grain against robbers. (Remember Ruth took place in the days of the Judges, so guards were needed.) At that point, Ruth could slip over to where Boaz was sleeping and do what Naomi had told her to do.

1. Read Ruth 3 as an overview and then answer these questions.

    A. Describe Naomi's plan (Ruth 3:1–4).

    B. Describe what happened at the threshing room floor (Ruth 3:5–15).

    C. Describe the interaction between Ruth and Naomi upon Ruth's return (Ruth 3:16–18).

2. Read Ruth 3:1–2.

    A. How has Naomi always addressed her daughters-in-law? (Now, again, in Ruth 2:11–12.) How is this significant?

    B. Find two phrases in verse 1 that describe Naomi's motivation.

    C. One of the strongest characteristics of a woman of love is that she plans good and then carries it out. How could you do this today?

    D. Of what facts does Naomi remind Ruth in verse 2?

DAY 2

Friendly Persuasion

A case can be made scripturally for the man to be the pursuer just as Christ is the pursuer, and for the woman to respond just as the bride of Christ responds to Christ. The gentle and quiet spirit that is so precious to God in a woman (1 Pet. 3:4) seems an antithesis to the aggressive woman who takes the initiative by calling, e-mailing, or simply asking him out.

So what are we to do with this story of Naomi instructing Ruth to go to Boaz in the middle of the night and making it known that she wants him to cover her, a symbolic way of expressing a desire for marriage?

This story *must* be read in the context of the culture.

3. What does Naomi say to Ruth when she discovers that she "happened" to glean in the field of Boaz? How exactly does she describe Boaz in Ruth 2:20?

Naomi does not say that Boaz is first in line as the kinsman-redeemer, instead she notes he is "a" kinsman-redeemer to them, or, as the *King James Version* puts it, "one of our next kinsman." As the story unfolds, we will discover that the "kinsman-redeemer" who is closest to the family bloodline is not a man of integrity. The fact that Ruth "happened" in the field of Boaz, who was so kind to her, is significant to Naomi. She seems to see

God's redemptive hand. Boaz has indeed been the pursuer by being so kind to Ruth, and yet he may be hesitant for he knows (as does Naomi) that he is not first in line.

4. When Ruth does go to Boaz, what does he tell her in Ruth 3:12–13? Why might Boaz, therefore, have needed some encouragement from Ruth?

5. What instructions does Naomi give to Ruth in Ruth 3:3–4?

J. Vernon McGee explains that after Boaz had shown an interest in Ruth, according to the Mosaic system (Deut. 25:5–10), it was incumbent upon Ruth to make a definite move. If she didn't, it would have constituted a rejection of Boaz as a suitor. When Ruth pulled the end of the long mantle that was covering Boaz over herself, she was letting him know she wanted his shelter and protection. "This was a symbolic and modest way of telling Boaz that she would be willing to accept him as the *'goel'* to take Mahlon's place in a leviritic marriage."[1]

Because Boaz was not first in line, the right legal response would be for Boaz to offer the nearer kinsman the opportunity to redeem Ruth. He does so very skillfully, as we will see, and Ruth is refused. Then Boaz is free and clear to marry Ruth.

Naomi's plan is to show Boaz that Ruth wants him to fulfill the role of kinsman-redeemer. It is a bit risky; Ruth doesn't know how Boaz will respond.

6. How does Ruth respond to Naomi's plan (Ruth 3:5)? How is this consistent with what we have seen in Ruth's actions previously?

Naomi's plan is friendly persuasion. She wants Ruth to go secretly so that Boaz will not be pressured. If he refuses Ruth, no one needs to know. But he won't. Naomi discerns he is drawn to Ruth. Women have intuition about these things. But it is gentle. It is also a form of a word picture, which is an effective way of tapping into the male right brain. In *The Language of Love,* Gary Smalley and John Trent explain that it is effective to use word pictures in persuading others, particularly men.

For example, when the prophet Nathan came to David after David's sins of adultery and murder, instead of stating David's sin outright, he told him a story of a man who had only one little lamb, and how that lamb had been stolen by a man who had much, much more. David was angry and then was told that that "he was the man." In this situation, Ruth lies down and pulls a little of the mantle over her, symbolically showing her desire to be "covered," to be protected in marriage by Boaz. She melts the man's heart.

7. Read Ruth 3:7–11

A. In what mood was Boaz when he went to sleep? Do you think Naomi knew this would be the case?

B. Why is it wise to think about timing when we approach someone with a request?

C. Look carefully at verse 7 and then describe how Ruth came to Boaz.

D. How does Boaz feel in verse 8?

E. What does his question in verse 9 tell you?

F. When coming to someone with a request, it is important for you to speak gently, but also to be direct enough so that they know exactly what you want to happen. How do you see Ruth doing this in verse 9?

G. How does Boaz respond in verses 10–13? Find everything you can.

H. What additional reason, besides not being first in line, can you see in his reply that might have caused Boaz to be reluctant to pursue Ruth more aggressively?

8. When you approach someone with something that is important to you, how might you learn from Naomi about how to be gentle and effective?

DAY 3

A Woman of Excellence

Though it surprises me, some have accused Ruth of sexual immorality. They say that because she spent the night, that she and Boaz had sexual intercourse. They did not. Cyril Barber explains: "The Hebrew word *lun,* 'to pass the night,' has latent within it the passage of time and does not concern itself with the manner in which the time was spent. If Boaz and Ruth had engaged in sexual relations on the threshing floor then *sakab,* 'to lie (together), to sleep (together)' would have been used. *Lun* is a word devoid of sexual connotations."[2]

9. Do you think Boaz would have called Ruth "a woman of excellence" had she come to seduce him sexually? Why or why not?

Later, after Boaz has married Ruth, a very different phrase is used, implying much more than the passage of time (see Ruth 4:13).

10. Look ahead to Ruth 4:13 and structure this verse as you did in chapter 6, day 2.

11. What do you see from structuring the above verse?

12. The phrase "went into" or "he [or she] came into" is used to discreetly describe sexual intercourse. How is it used in the following historical passages?

   A. Genesis 29:21

   B. 2 Samuel 11:4

   C. Esther 2:12–14 (occurs twice in this passage)

13. Contrast Ruth 3:13 with Ruth 4:13

It is always important to look at a passage within its cultural context, or it may be misinterpreted. For a woman today to go to a man at night and pull the blanket he is sleeping under partially over herself implies something far different than it did in this cultural setting.

In Old Testament days, and even in many cultures today, parents arranged the marriages of their children. If you've seen *Fiddler on the Roof*, you may remember the father's shock when the daughters wanted to choose their own husbands. This was not fitting or respectful! Here, in Ruth, Naomi was taking the role of Ruth's parent in a culturally appropriate way of arranging her marriage.

14. How do you see Naomi's concern for the remarriage of her daughters-in-law in the following passages?

    A. Ruth 1:8–9

    B. Ruth 3:1

15. The book of Ruth took place "in the days when the judges ruled." Not all young people respected the culture of the day, but instead chose to do what "seemed right to them." Read Judges 14:1–3.

    A. What did Samson want and why? There is a strong sexual connotation in the word pleases. It is the same word used in Esther when the foolish advisors arrange an immoral "beauty" contest for the new queen, looking for a woman who would "please" the decadent king.

    B. How did Samson's parents respond, and why? (v. 3)

16. Contrast Samson's response to his parents with Ruth's response to Naomi in Ruth 3:5.

17. How does Boaz affirm Ruth in Ruth 3:10? How does this again show that she was respecting Naomi and the culture—unlike many of her peers who were "doing what was right in their own eyes?"

18. If someone were to tell you Ruth must have slept with Boaz that night at the threshing room floor, how would you respond? How would you support your answer with Scripture?

DAY 4

· ·

Take Your Maidservant under Your Wing

The concept of a husband protecting or "covering" his bride is also important to understand or you will not understand this scene at the threshing room floor. God has called husbands—not just in that culture, but yesterday, today, and tomorrow—to protect and provide for their wives, for they are to be reflective of Christ, who covers His bride with protection and provision. The Hebrew word for *covering* and *wing* is the same. Husbands are to bring wives under their protection, under their "wings," just as God brings His bride under His wings.

19. How has Boaz demonstrated to Ruth (and to Naomi) that he is a man of excellence who treats women well? `

A. Ruth 2:8–9

B. Ruth 2:14–16

20. What exhortations does God give to husbands in the following passages?

A. Ephesians 5:25

B. Ephesians 5:28

C. 1 Peter 3:7

D. 1 Timothy 5:8

There is a fascinating passage in Malachi in which Israelite husbands have become attracted to younger pagan women and have cast their wives aside, without even a certificate of divorce. (A woman without a certificate of divorce could not remarry and was reduced to begging or prostitution.) It is like the spirit in the days of Judges when they were doing what seemed right in their own eyes and were blind to God. They were still going to church (temple, actually) as usual, acting as if they have done nothing wrong, and were still offering sacrifices to God.

Read Malachi 2:13–16 in the English Standard Version:

And this second thing you do. You cover the LORD's altar with tears, with weeping and groaning because he no longer regards the offering or accepts it with favor from your hand. But you say, Why does he not? Because the LORD was witness between you and the wife of your youth, to whom you have been faithless, though she is your companion and your wife by covenant. Did he not make them one, with a portion of the Spirit in their union? And what was the one God seeking? Godly offspring. So guard yourselves in your spirit, and let none of you be faithless to the wife of your youth. For the man who hates and divorces, says the LORD, the God of Israel, covers his garment with violence, says the LORD of hosts. So guard yourselves in your spirit, and do not be faithless.

21. Meditate on the above.

    A. Why are the men of Malachi weeping and groaning (v. 13)?

    B. What answer does Malachi give, from the Lord, to the husband's question, "Why does he not?"

    C. List everything you learn about marriage from verse 15.

    D. What warning does God give to the man who hates and divorces his wife?

Sometimes verse 16 is translated, "I [meaning God] hate divorce." God does hate divorce, but he certainly doesn't hate the victim, and there often is a victim. He hates what it does to both partners, to the children, and to the world. Sometimes this phrase is taken out of context and directed to the victim who has been abandoned by an unfaithful spouse. That is a cruel misapplication. The phrase "the Lord … covers his garment with violence" is another difficult phrase to translate, but there is a play on words. Men are to cover their wives with protection, not violence or treachery. If they do not cover them with protection, then God will cover them with violence.

22. If a woman has been abandoned by her husband, how might the above words from the Lord give her comfort?

Read the Lord's condemnation in verse 14 as it is translated in the *New Living Translation*:

You cry out, "Why has the LORD abandoned us?" I'll tell you why! Because the LORD witnessed the vows you and your wife made to each other on your wedding day when you were young. But you have been disloyal to her, though she remained your faithful companion, the wife of your marriage vows.

Even though husbands may walk out, parents may fail to love, and friends may betray, God is a faithful Bridegroom, a loving Father, and a Friend who is closer than a brother. He will never leave us nor forsake us.

23. Read Ruth 3:11–15.

    A. What does Boaz tell Ruth not to do in verse 11? In what ways does he reassure her?

    B. What obstacle does Boaz tell Ruth about, and what is his two-part plan?

    C. What hope can you read between the lines in the response of Boaz?

    D. How is Boaz careful to avoid even the appearance of immorality for Ruth (Ruth 3:14)?

    E. How does Boaz provide for Ruth (and Naomi) again (Ruth 3:15)?
    Can you say your memory verse by heart?

DAY 5

How Did It Go, My Daughter?

She's dying to know. The matchmaker has waited all night for a report. And like any woman, she wants details.

When Naomi asks Ruth about her night, Ruth tells her everything. (How many daughters-in-law do that?) Each of these women sought the other's best. Each has learned to trust the other.

Then Naomi encourages Ruth, being confident Boaz will do the right thing and that the matter will be settled. Naomi, who is restored, is back in her role as a mentor, a confidante, and encourager.

24. Read Ruth 3:16–18.

    A. What question from Naomi reveals that it is still dark?

    B. How much did Ruth tell Naomi?

C. What detail does Ruth add to show that Boaz was thinking of Naomi, as well?

25. Remembering the pictures of famine and of barrenness, how has this changed by the close of chapter 3?

26. If you have a mother-in-law, how willing are you to raise her to a new level of intimacy? If not, is it because of pride or a lack of forgiveness toward past hurts or some-thing else? Explain.

27. What wise advice does Naomi give to Ruth in Ruth 3:18?

28. Sometimes we take action before we have waited on the Lord. Why is this foolish? Is there an application to your life?

Review your memory passage from each of the first three chapters of Ruth.

PRAYER TIME

An essential for effective prayer is honesty. Vulnerably lift up a need in your life, either for your own walk or another area that is of concern to you. Let your sisters support you with sentences of earnest prayer.

Eight

Better than Seven Sons!

My grandmother Brown had seven sons. She seemed to run out of names, for she named a couple of sons Jim. I asked her, "Grandmother, why did you name more than one son Jim?"

She said, "Good name, Jim." (She was not a woman of many words!)

My grandmother always hoped for a little girl, but instead, God gave her seven sons. I wonder if she knew that in biblical days, a perfect family was considered one with seven sons.

This adds light to what the women of Bethlehem say to Naomi at the close of the book of Ruth: "Your daughter-in-law is better to you than seven sons."

Ruth certainly was a woman of love, but she wasn't alone. She had a God who wooed her, a mother-in-law who mentored her, a man who protected her, and a fellowship of believers who prayed for her.

Memory Work

Spend time learning your final memory verse, Ruth 4:15:

> *He will renew your life and sustain you in your old age. For your daughter-in-law, who loves you and who is better to you than seven sons, has given him birth.*

WARMUP

Think of a very specific prayer you dared to pray and saw answered. In one breath, share what it was.

DAY 1

● ●

True Religion

The Lord set up laws to care for the widow, the stranger, and the poor in the Old Testament. That was part of the Old Covenant. We are not under the Law today, but there is a New Covenant. The Holy Spirit is in our hearts to help us do what we could not do because of our sinful nature. The Law, however, can help us understand not only God's heart, but our need for the Spirit to help us to carry out His heart.

1. Read Deuteronomy 25:5–10.

    A. What duty is given to a surviving "brother" of a widow according to verse 5?

    B. Why, according to verse 6?

    C. If the "brother" does not do his duty, what instructions are given to the widow according to verse 7?

    D. Does the above give you any light as to why Naomi came up with her plan?

    E. What are the elders to do, according to verse 8, if the widow does come forward?

    F. What disgraceful ceremony is to be performed to expose the lack of compassion and integrity toward the man who refuses his duty?

2. What law is explained in Leviticus 25:25? How might this relate to our story?

3. Though we are not under the Law, God's heart can be seen in the Law, and we are to be His heart in this world. How does James define true religion in James 1:27?

4. How might you apply James 1:27 in your life?

DAY 2

A True Prince Charming

Every Cinderella story needs an obstacle and a Prince Charming who is able to surmount that obstacle. We surely see that in the closing chapter of Ruth. There is a huge problem, but a capable "Prince Charming," and a very happy ending.

The problem? There is a kinsman-redeemer who is a closer blood relative. He is not a man of integrity, but he could stand between the union of Ruth and Boaz if he chose. This would be disastrous, not only for Ruth and Boaz, but for Naomi and for future generations. But God is not going to let this happen, and He is going to use Boaz.

Sing hymns and complete your memorization.

5. Read Ruth 4:1 ask the who, what, when, why questions to help you see:

   A. Who was involved

   B. What happened

   C. When did it happen

   D. Why was Boaz doing this

6. Read Ruth 4:2–8.

   A. Why do you think Boaz asked 10 elders to come to the gate with him?

There wasn't a legal requirement for the number of witnesses (though 10 men made up a quorum for worship), but it was wise to have witnesses, for in a rural culture, the use of writing was limited.

   B. What information does Boaz give the nearest kinsman?

   C. How do you see tact, faith, and honesty in the words of Boaz?

D. What is the unnamed kinsman's first response?   He is probably unnamed out of kindness from the author, who chose not to have his selfishness memorialized.

E. What other responsibilities come along with the land (v. 5)?

F. Now, what is the nearer kinsman's second response, and what reason does he give for refusing Ruth (v. 6)?

In all probability the nearer kinsman thought his responsibility was to Naomi, and that since she was too old to have a son, there would never be anyone to take the land from him. However, Naomi has transferred her right to Ruth, and Ruth is young enough to have a son who would grow up to inherit the land. Boaz has revealed, before 10 witnesses, the motivation of the nearer kinsman. He is not interested in caring for these widows. He simply wanted the land. Ruth has been rescued from a disastrous marriage.

G. What ceremony happens in verses 7 and 8? How is it significant?

7. In the close of chapter 3 and the opening of 4, what evidence can you find for quiet confidence (as opposed to panic) as these three godly individuals faced this rather frightening obstacle?

A. How do you see calm in Naomi?

B. In Ruth?

C. In Boaz?

Manipulation is the reverse of faith. If God is real and personal, then we don't need to manipulate. We do what God leads us to do and no more. Then we wait and trust that God will do what is best for us or our children. A woman of love doesn't manipulate but trusts God and does what is right.

8. Contrast the responses of the following individuals in Ruth: What is God's response to them?

   A. Elimelech and Boaz

   B. Orpah and Ruth

   C. Boaz and the nearer kinsman

9. As you examine your own heart, do you live by faith or fear? By manipulation or by honesty? Be still before God. What do you see and how will you respond?

DAY 3
. . . .

We Are All Witnesses!

Boaz can hardly contain his exuberance. Though the Law gave him the right to spit in the nearer kinsman's selfish face, Boaz is too happy for spitting. He probably came closer to hugging him!

And it isn't just Boaz who is celebrating. The whole town seems to be rejoicing. They loved Boaz, they loved Ruth, and they loved Naomi. What a sweet scene of the fellowship of believers. They belong to a God who bends down and answers prayer. Truly, this is a joyful wedding.

10. Read Ruth 4:9–10.

   A. Whose land did Boaz buy and from whom?

B. Whom has he acquired as his wife?

C. Whose memory will be perpetuated throughout Israel?

D. How do you see exuberance in this speech?

11. How had the whole town felt when Naomi first returned (Ruth 1:19)?

12. What did all of Boaz's fellow townsmen know about Ruth (Ruth 3:11)?

13. What evidence do you see that there were more than 10 witnesses here (Ruth 4:11)?

14. Meditate on the very specific prayer by the townspeople in Ruth 4:11–12.
    A. In what way do these townspeople ask God to make Ruth like Rachel and Leah? (Look carefully!)

    B. What else do they pray for in verse 11?

15. In verse 12, they mention Judah, who, like the nearer kinsman, stands in an unfavorable light when compared to Boaz. Read the story in Genesis 38:6–30.
    A. What happened to Judah's first son and why (vv. 6–7)?

B. What happened to Judah's second son and why (vv. 8–10)?

C. Why do you think it was wicked of Onan to spill his seed?

Some have called this the sin of contraception. I see it as the sin of selfishness, rooted in a lack of faith. Onan did not honor the moral law of God, nor his father, nor his brother, nor his brother's widow because he didn't see anything in this arrangement for himself.

D. What lie did Judah then tell Tamar? What motivated his lie (v. 11)?

E. How did God show Himself shrewd to Judah (vv. 12–30)?

F. How does Boaz compare favorably to Judah?

Carrying on the name of the late kinsman was voluntary. Neither Judah nor the nearer kinsman had to do it. To do so was a sacrifice and an act of faith. It showed *hesed* (unfailing love) and honored God. Boaz chose, because of love, to be a redeemer.

Can you say Ruth 4:15 by heart?

DAY 4
• •

Bridal Showers, Weddings, Baby Showers

Marriage is God's holy ordinance, and a marriage (or a divorce) impacts many more people than just the bride and groom. Therefore a wedding should involve the community as it does here. The enormous opportunity of having believers pray for the couple should be seized (bridal showers are another opportunity). Then, in the future, the community of believers has a continued responsibility to support the marriage through prayer and encouragement.

David Atkinson says,

> *In our day, marriage is coming to be thought of by some only as a private alliance*

between two people, to be made (and even terminated) as they wish, by their private choice. But society has always had an interest in the formation of a new pair bond, and the growth of a new family unit in society.[1]

16. What can you glean as the purpose for involving the community of believers in a wedding from Ruth 4:9–12?

Weddings are important to God. Jesus began His ministry at a wedding and will close with a wedding. For when He comes back, He is coming as a Bridegroom for His bride. Weddings should be both a festive and a serious time, as that great day will be.

17. How might an earthly wedding be a reflection of the day Jesus comes back for His bride? Much of our tradition is based on the symbolism of Scripture, including a white wedding gown, a trumpet, a wedding banquet, and so forth. (Do some digging with your concordance!)

18. According to Ephesians 5:21–32, how can an earthly marriage be a reflection of the relationship between Jesus and true believers (the church)?

19. How do you see this in the relationship of Boaz and Ruth?

20. If you were helping to plan a shower or a wedding, what would be some festive and God-honoring ideas? What might you learn from the example of the townspeople in Ruth?

21. How might you pray for the bride and groom scripturally? For a mother-to-be?

DAY 5

. . . .

Naomi has a Son!

The women of Bethlehem tell Naomi that Ruth is better to her than seven sons! Perhaps they remember that when Naomi returned to Bethlehem with Ruth, she said, "I've come back empty."

Naomi is not empty. Ruth has been an amazing gift. Now, the friends are at the home during the birth of Naomi's grandson. Intriguingly, they name the baby! They name him "Obed," which means "servant," and in Ruth 4:14–15, the women say,

> Praise be to the LORD, who this day has not left you without a kinsman-redeemer. May he become famous throughout Israel! He will renew your life and sustain you in your old age. For your daughter-in-law, who loves you and who is better to you than seven sons, has given him birth.

Better than seven sons! What an accolade! A perfect family in Israel was seven sons. In cultures where men are valued more than women, rich more than poor, God looks on the heart. And to the faithful He shows Himself faithful.

Then Ruth takes this baby, for whom she has waited so long, and puts him in Naomi's empty arms. As the godly Boaz took both women into his home, Naomi is alone no more. Her empty arms are full, she is embraced by a family and by the community of believers, and her future is hopeful. What a lovely family portrait showing the power of God to the faithful with which to close this book of *hesed*.

Read Ruth 4:13–22.

22. How do you see the prayers of the believers at the wedding being answered in verse 13? In verses 21–22?

23. Using just the names in the last two verses of Ruth, trace the bloodline from Boaz and Ruth to Jesus.

24. If you have friends struggling with infertility, how could you help them? (If someone in your group has experienced this personally, encourage her to share what helps and what does not help.)

25. What would be a wise way to pray?

Occasionally when touching on this subject in my speaking, the Spirit prompts me to pray, from the podium, for those experiencing this very painful situation. Often I pray that God will either give them the desire of their heart or change the desire of their heart (Ps. 37:4). Recently a woman came up to me who had been present when I prayed that way five years earlier. She said, "I had had six miscarriages. When you prayed that way, suddenly an overwhelming peace came over me. I have not been able to conceive again, but I have had a peace. I am not imagining it, neither could I have drummed it up. That peace is a gift from God."

26. Describe the praise, prayer, and prophecy of the women at the house that day. What stands out to you and why?

27. This story also illustrates Psalm 68:6. Explain how.

28. If you have a husband and children, have you "adopted" any people who are single? If so, share something about it.

29. How do the women of Bethlehem give a gentle rebuke to Naomi (Ruth 4:15)?

30. What have you seen in particular in the life of Ruth which you admire? (Instead of just saying "love" or "faith," be passionate and specific. For example, "I'll never forget how she kept on loving Naomi even when Naomi hurt her feelings!")

31. How do you desire to follow Ruth's example in your own life?

PRAYER TIME

Have each woman, one by one, kneel in the center of a circle. (For time's sake, you may want to break into circles of four or five.) As she kneels, she should share her answer to question 28. All place their hands on her and pray silently. Two or three should pray aloud with sentence prayers. When there is silence, she should rise and another woman should take her place.

Nine

I Will Sing of My Redeemer

At the close of the story, the women friends of Naomi surround her as she cradles Obed and say, "Praise be to the LORD, who this day has not left you without a kinsman-redeemer" (Ruth 4:14).

We too should cry, "Thanks be to God, who has not left us without a Kinsman-Redeemer!" Like Ruth, we were aliens, "foreigners to the covenants of the promise, without hope and without God in the world" (Eph. 2:12). But because God loved us so, He sent a Kinsman-Redeemer to earth, so that now in Christ Jesus we "who once were far away have been brought near through the blood of Christ" (Eph. 2:13).

WARMUP

God places great value on the *family* of God. We are to value our relationships as sisters in Christ. In one breath, share one way the sisters in this small group have blessed you.

DAY I

Jesus in the Old Concealed, Jesus in the New Revealed

The Old Testament is like a picture book. But when we get to the New Testament, suddenly, we see the captions. When we realize, for example, that Boaz is a picture of Jesus as our Kinsman-Redeemer, the story penetrates our hearts anew. When I consider the multilayered book of Ruth, full of pictures that have so much more significance on a spiritual level, I am in awe. Pictures of barren land made fruitful, of empty arms made full, of outcasts redeemed, and of ashes turned to beauty. I often think, *How did You do that, Lord? I know this story truly happened, so how did You make it so full of symbolism?* When I reflect on the magnitude of God, I echo the thoughts of David in Psalm 8:3–4:

> *When I consider your heavens, the work of your fingers, the moon and the stars, which you have set in place, what is man that you are mindful of him?*

Yet, the good news is that God is mindful of us. Jesus was willing to leave His throne in heaven. He was willing to take on the form of man, the form of a servant, to be our Kinsman. He paid dearly to redeem us, not with silver or gold, but with His precious blood (1 Pet. 1:18–19). Praise be to God, who has not left us without a Kinsman-Redeemer!

You should be able to remember the heart of each chapter in Ruth by repeating your memory work. If you look closely at your verses, you will also see symbolism. If Ruth is speaking, consider how she reflects us as individual believers, and us together as the Bride of Christ. If Boaz is speaking, consider how he reflects Jesus.

1. Write down your memory verses and then any symbolism you see.

    A. Ruth 1

    B. Ruth 2

    C. Ruth 3

    D. Ruth 4

2. How do you see Jesus glimmering in the person of Boaz in the following?

    A. Ruth 2:1

    B. Ruth 2:8–9

    C. Ruth 2:14–16

    D. Ruth 3:11

    E. Ruth 3:15

    F. Ruth 4:9

DAY 2

Jesus Our Kinsman

The book of Ruth shows the strong sense of family solidarity among the people of Yahweh. They had a duty to care for each other. The law of the "kinsman-redeemer" reflected that.

Jesus became one of us, and if we have trusted in His blood sacrifice, He is "not ashamed to call them brothers" (Heb. 2:11). J. Vernon McGee says this puts a heart into redemption.

> *A mother is willing to sacrifice herself for the child at her bosom because the little one is flesh of her flesh…. Blood relationship begets in the heart an affection and love that is sometimes beyond human comprehension.*[1]

Jesus almost invariably described Himself on earth as the "Son of Man." He is our brother, our Kinsman.

3. Think of a blood relative to whom you are close. Describe your bond.

4. With this in mind, what does it mean to you that Jesus became your Kinsman?

Read Ruth 2:13.

In the King James Version, the above verse says, "for that thou hast comforted me, and for that thou hast spoken friendly unto thine handmaid, though I be not like unto one of thine handmaidens." It overwhelms me personally when Jesus "speaks friendly to me." He is so holy and I am so sinful, yet He calls me, as Boaz did with Ruth, "My daughter" (Ruth 2:8; 3:10).

5. If possible, share a time when you sensed that Jesus "spoke friendly" to you or when you sensed He was treating you like "a daughter."

6. Read Hebrews 2 prayerfully.

    A. What passage from Psalms is repeated in verses 6–8?

B. What do we learn about Jesus becoming our Kinsman in verses 9–12?

C. What are some of the reasons Jesus became our Kinsman according to verses 14–18?

Personal Action Assignment

Jesus understands your weaknesses, because He shared in your humanity. Pray through Hebrews 4:15–16 in thanksgiving. Then tell Jesus your weaknesses and ask Him for grace to change.

DAY 3

Jesus Our Redeemer

Ruth was helpless, outcast, under the curse. As a Moabitess, she was not allowed to enter the assembly of the Lord even unto the tenth generation (Deut. 23:3). But the curse is broken. She enters in, becomes an ancestor of Christ, and has her name listed in the genealogy of Christ (Matt. 1:5). Why? Because Ruth is no longer a Moabitess. Ruth is redeemed, covered in righteousness. The book that began with famine and death ends with plenty and new life.

The baby born to Ruth and Boaz will become the grandfather of David. And out of David, and the city of David, will come forth one whose origins have been from of old, from everlasting.

7. Describe the helplessness of Ruth as a Moabite widow.

8. Describe our helplessness before a Holy God and our bondage in sin (Rom. 3:23; John 8:34).

9. Explain how the transaction Boaz made to redeem Ruth was a public transaction (Ruth 4).

10. Explain how the transaction Jesus made to redeem us was a public transaction. (See John 3:14; 12:32–33.)

11. Explain how the transaction Boaz made to redeem Ruth was costly (Ruth 4:9).

12. Explain how the transaction Jesus made to redeem us was much more costly. (See 1 Pet. 1:18–19.)

13. What did Naomi gain because Boaz paid the price of redemption?

14. What do we gain because Jesus paid the price for our redemption? (See Col. 1:12–14.)

DAY 4

Hesed *in Naomi and Ruth*

The book of Ruth has been called the book of *hesed*, of "unfailing love." There are two concepts intertwined in this great Hebrew word: *kindness* (or mercy) and *steadfastness*. *Hesed* is what every single person desires from God and from their loved ones (Prov. 19:22a). We want our loved ones to be kind and merciful to us and to never give up on us. God always gives *hesed*, and He longs for us to give it to one another, but it is actually very rare (Prov. 20:6). In the days of the judges there were very few who showed *hesed*. But God has always had a remnant, and shining in those dark days were Naomi, Ruth, and Boaz.

Naomi is the central character in the book of Ruth. Everything and everyone revolves around her. Elimelech is defined as "Naomi's husband," Orpah and Ruth as "Naomi's daughters-in-law," and Boaz as "Naomi's relative." *Hesed* begins with Naomi in the opening of the book as she gives this unfailing love to her Moabite daughters-in-law. And *hesed* comes back full circle to Naomi at the close of the book in the idyllic scene with her friends, family, and newborn grandson.

Meditate on God's *hesed* (unfailing love) by singing "Great Is Thy Faithfulness" (see Hymns Index).

15. *Hesed* is used to describe the love of the Lord. How do you see both kindness and steadfastness in Lamentations 3:22–23?

16. Which aspect of *hesed* do you see most clearly personified in Naomi—kindness or steadfastness? Explain.

17. Kindness is voluntary. Naomi did not have to accept her Moabite daughters-in-law, but she did. Why was this remarkable?

18. Review the evidence from Ruth 1 that Naomi loved and blessed her daughters-in-law.

There is great power in the kind of love demonstrated in the book of Ruth. Likewise, there can be great harm wrought through the lack of *hesed*. (Philip Yancey calls this "ungrace.") When we give "ungrace," we bring great pain to ourselves, our relationships, and to future generations. It's painful to forgive when we have been wronged. "The only thing harder than forgiveness is the alternative."[2]

19. How was Naomi blessed by giving grace? How did it eventually lead to her restoration?

20. What might have happened to Naomi had she refused to embrace Ruth and Orpah? What do you learn from this?

21. Are there people in your life to whom you have difficulty giving grace?

Specifically how could you give them grace?

22. What will you remember about Naomi's model of *hesed*?

The example of Ruth comes to my mind nearly every day of my life. I am so thankful for her example of steadfast love and its power in breaking down walls. When I am rejected, whether it is by a daughter who is dealing with the pain of spending her childhood in an orphanage or by a friend who is dealing with a storm within, I remember Ruth. Five times Naomi rejected her. Never does Ruth lash out. Never does Ruth retreat. She just keeps on loving, and in due time, she sees a harvest.

The hardest time to give unfailing love is when we feel unappreciated, yet, if we do not give up, we will bear fruit.

23. Describe the warning and the promise given in Galatians 6:7–10.

24. How is Ruth an example of the above promise?

25. Review Ruth 1 and find the five rejections from Naomi. Describe Ruth's response. Why do you think Ruth was able to respond as she did?

Not even Abraham's leap of faith surpasses this decision of Ruth's. And there is more. Not only has Ruth broken with family, country and faith, but she has also reversed sexual allegiance. A young woman has committed herself to the life of an old woman rather than to the search for a husband…. One female has chosen another female in a world where life depends upon men. There is no more radical decision in all the memories of Israel.[3]

26. How do you respond when someone rejects you?

27. What could you learn from Ruth?

28. List all the ways in which Ruth filled up Naomi's empty arms. Give verse references.

29. List all the ways God blessed Ruth for her unfailing love. Give verse references.

30. What do you think you will remember from the example of Ruth?

DAY 5

Hesed in Boaz

The magnanimity of Boaz knows no bounds. He does not have to do what he freely chooses to do, which is to provide for Ruth, protect her, marry her, and embrace not only her, but her mother-in-law. A key aspect of *hesed* is that it is voluntary, which is what makes it so amazing.

Glimmering beneath the figure of Boaz is our wonderful Lord. He did not have to leave His throne in heaven, but He chose to come to earth and become our Kinsman. Likewise, He did not have to die for us, but He chose to be our Redeemer.

Prepare your heart by singing "My Redeemer" (see Hymns Index).

31. How did you see unfailing love in Boaz? Give verse references.

32. How did God bless Boaz because of his unfailing love?

33. What do you think you will remember from the example of Boaz?

34. How do you see Jesus glimmering beneath the figure of Boaz?

35. Describe the song that is sung about our Kinsman-Redeemer in Revelation 5:9–10.

36. Write down several ways your life is different because you have a Kinsman-Redeemer. (From what has He freed you? What have you inherited?)

37. Write down five blessings you have received from any of the following:
    • Truths God impressed on your heart from the life of Naomi

    • Truths God impressed on your heart from the life of Ruth

    • Truths God impressed on your heart from the life of Boaz

    • Qualities of God that have become more vibrant to you because of the book of Ruth

    • Changes you have seen in your life as a result of this study

    • Specific ways women in this group have blessed you

    • Answers to prayer during the study

    • Any other benefits for which you wish to praise the Lord!

PRAYER TIME

Place a punch bowl half full of water in the middle of the room. Give each woman five smooth pebbles. David, Ruth's great-grandson, killed the giant Goliath with five smooth stones. There are giants of despair, discouragement, and division that threaten our spiritual lives, but we can slay them with praise. The discussion facilitator can lead this time of praise by reading through the list in question 37: "Bless the Lord, O my soul, and forget not all His benefits. How did He minister to you from the life of Naomi?"

Then women can share, putting their pebbles in the water as they do. For example, one might say, "I bless the Lord for Naomi's example of grace toward her Moabite daughters-in-law."

Then, when the sharing is complete, the discussion facilitator can say, "Bless the Lord, O my soul, and forget not all His benefits. How did He minister to you from the life of Ruth?" And so forth.

Memory Verses

WEEKS 1–3 (Key passage for Ruth 1)

And Ruth said, Intreat me not to leave thee, or to return from following after thee: for whither thou goest, I will go; and where thou lodgest, I will lodge: thy people shall be my people, and thy God my God: Where thou diest, will I die, and there will I be buried: the LORD do so to me, and more also, if ought but death part thee and me.
Ruth 1:16–17 (KJV)

WEEKS 4–6 (Key passage for Ruth 2)

At this, she bowed down with her face to the ground. She exclaimed, "Why have I found such favor in your eyes that you notice me—a foreigner?" Boaz replied, "I've been told all about what you have done for your mother-in-law since the death of your husband—how you left your father and mother and your homeland and came to live with a people you did not know before. May the LORD repay you for what you have done. May you be richly rewarded by the LORD, the God of Israel, under whose wings you have come to take refuge." "May I continue to find favor in your eyes, my lord," she said. "You have given me comfort and have spoken kindly to your servant—though I do not have the standing of one of your servant girls."
Ruth 2:10–13

WEEK 7 (Key passage for Ruth 3)

"Who are you?" he asked. "I am your servant Ruth," she said. "Spread the corner of your garment over me, since you are a kinsman-redeemer."
Ruth 3:9

WEEK 8 (Key passage for Ruth 4)

He will renew your life and sustain you in your old age. For your daughter-in-law, who loves you and who is better to you than seven sons, has given him birth.
Ruth 4:15

222

My Redeemer

Philip P. Bliss   James McGranahan

1. I will sing of my Re-deem-er, And His won-drous love to me;
2. I will tell the won-drous sto-ry, How my lost es-tate to save,
3. I will praise my dear Re-deem-er, His tri-um-phant pow'r I'll tell,
4. I will sing of my Re-deem-er, And His heav'n-ly love to me;

On the cru-el cross He suf-fered, From the curse to set me free.
In His bound-less love and mer-cy, He the ran-som free-ly gave.
How the vic-to-ry He giv-eth O-ver sin, and death, and hell.
He from death to life hath bro't me, Son of God with Him to be.

CHORUS

Sing, oh, sing . . . . of my Re-deem-er,
of my Re-deem-er, Sing, oh, sing of my Re-deem-er,

With His blood . . . . He pur-chased me, ...
He pur-chased me, With His blood He pur-chased me,

On the cross . . . . He sealed my par-don,
He sealed my par-don, On the cross He sealed my par-don,

Paid the debt, ... and made me free. . . . .
and made me free, and made me free.

For the Beauty of the Earth

FOLLIOTT S. PIERPOINT

ARR. FROM CONRAD KOCHER

1. For the beau-ty of the earth, For the glo-ry of the skies,
2. For the won-der of each hour Of the day and of the night,
3. For the joy of hu-man love, Broth-er, sis-ter, par-ent, child,
4. For Thy Church that ev-er-more Lift-eth ho-ly hands a-bove,

For the love which from our birth O-ver and a-round us lies:
Hill and vale and tree and flower, Sun and moon and stars of light:
Friends on earth, and friends a-bove, For all gen-tle thoughts and mild:
Of-fering up on ev-ery shore Her pure sac-ri-fice of love:

Christ our God, to Thee we raise This our hymn of grate-ful praise.
Christ our God, to Thee we raise This our hymn of grate-ful praise.
Christ our God, to Thee we raise This our hymn of grate-ful praise.
Christ our God, to Thee we raise This our hymn of grate-ful praise.

The Solid Rock

EDWARD MOTE

WILLIAM B. BRADBURY

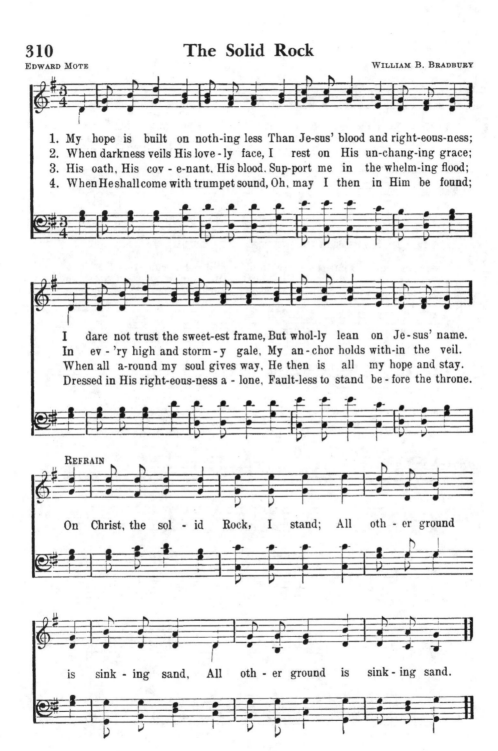

1. My hope is built on noth-ing less Than Je-sus' blood and right-eous-ness;
2. When darkness veils His love-ly face, I rest on His un-chang-ing grace;
3. His oath, His cov-e-nant, His blood, Sup-port me in the whelm-ing flood;
4. When He shall come with trumpet sound, Oh, may I then in Him be found;

I dare not trust the sweet-est frame, But whol-ly lean on Je-sus' name.
In ev-'ry high and storm-y gale, My an-chor holds with-in the veil.
When all a-round my soul gives way, He then is all my hope and stay.
Dressed in His right-eous-ness a-lone, Fault-less to stand be-fore the throne.

REFRAIN

On Christ, the sol-id Rock, I stand; All oth-er ground

is sink-ing sand, All oth-er ground is sink-ing sand.

Under His Wings

William O. Cushing

Ira D. Sankey

1. Un-der His wings I am safe-ly a-bid-ing; Tho' the night
2. Un-der His wings, what a ref-uge in sor-row! How the heart
3. Un-der His wings, O what pre-cious en-joy-ment! There will I

deep-ens and tem-pests are wild, Still I can trust Him; I
yearn-ing-ly turns to His rest! Oft-en when earth has no
hide till life's tri-als are o'er; Shel-tered, pro-tect-ed, no

know He will keep me; He has re-deemed me, and I am His child.
balm for my heal-ing, There I find com-fort, and there I am blest.
e-vil can harm me; Rest-ing in Je-sus I'm safe ev-er-more.

CHORUS

Un-der His wings, un-der His wings, Who from His love can sev-er?

Un-der His wings my soul shall a-bide, Safe-ly a-bide for-ev-er.

A Mighty Fortress Is Our God

MARTIN LUTHER
TR. BY FREDERICK H. HEDGE

MARTIN LUTHER

1. A might-y for-tress is our God, A bul-wark nev-er fail - ing;
2. Did we in our own strength confide, Our striv-ing would be los - ing;
3. And tho' this world, with dev-ils filled, Should threaten to un-do us;
4. That word a - bove all earthly pow'rs—No thanks to them—a-bid - eth:

Our help - er He, a - mid the flood Of mor-tal ills pre-vail - ing.
Were not the right Man on our side, The Man of God's own choos - ing.
We will not fear, for God hath willed His truth to tri-umph through us.
The Spir - it and the gifts are ours Thro' Him who with us sid - eth.

For still our an-cient foe Doth seek to work us woe; His craft and pow'r are
Dost ask who that may be? Christ Je-sus, it is He; Lord Sabaoth is His
The prince of darkness grim—We tremble not for him; His rage we can en-
Let goods and kin-dred go, This mor-tal life al - so; The bod - y they may

great, And, armed with cru-el hate, On earth is not his e - qual.
name, From age to age the same, And He must win the bat - tle.
dure, For lo! his doom is sure, One lit-tle word shall fell him.
kill: God's truth a-bid-eth still, His king-dom is for - ev - er.

Come, Ye Thankful People, Come

Henry Alford

George J. Elvey

1. Come, ye thank-ful peo-ple, come, Raise the song of har-vest-home:
2. All the world is God's own field, Fruit un-to His praise to yield;
3. For the Lord our God shall come, And shall take His har-vest home;
4. E-ven so, Lord, quick-ly come To Thy fi-nal har-vest-home;

All is safe-ly gath-ered in, Ere the win-ter storms be-gin;
Wheat and tares to-geth-er sown, Un-to joy or sor-row grown;
From His field shall in that day All of-fenc-es purge a-way;
Gath-er Thou Thy peo-ple in, Free from sor-row, free from sin;

God, our Ma-ker, doth pro-vide For our wants to be sup-plied:
First the blade, and then the ear, Then the full corn shall ap-pear:
Give His an-gels charge at last In the fire the tares to cast;
There, for-ev-er pu-ri-fied, In Thy pres-ence to a-bide:

Come to God's own tem-ple, come, Raise the song of har-vest-home.
Lord of har-vest, grant that we Wholesome grain and pure may be.
But the fruit-ful ears to store In His gar-ner ev-er-more.
Come, with all Thine an-gels, come, Raise the glo-rious har-vest-home.

Cover Me

Cover me, Lord, with your presence,
Cover me, Lord, with your righteousness.
Cover me, Lord, with your holiness,
Lord Jesus, cover me.

I need your protection from danger and harm,
Shelter me safe in your strong loving arms.
Help me to see there's no cause for alarm,
Lord Jesus, cover me.

Under your shadow I won't be afraid,
Cover me, Lord, till the storm blows away.
Then in the heat of a beautiful day,
Lord Jesus, cover me.

Leader's Helps for
A Woman of Love

1. Love in a Time of Famine

13. Help them see how rich with pictures Ruth is, remembering parallels between physical fruitfulness and spiritual fruitfulness, and physical emptiness and spiritual emptiness. These are just a few of the images to get you started—there are literally dozens. Ruth 1: "a famine in the land" (v. 1); "Am I going to have any more sons, who could become your husbands?" (v. 11);
"I am too old to have another husband" (v. 12);
"arriving in Bethlehem as the barley harvest was beginning" (v. 22).
Ruth 2: "Let me go to the fields and pick up the leftover grain" (v. 2); "went out and began to glean in the field behind the harvesters. And it turned out, she found herself working in a field belonging to Boaz" (v. 3).

2. Distorted Love

13. Ask them to be brief, sharing simply how Christ was made clear to them and how He changed their lives—in a sentence. You could go first to model clarity and brevity. For example, I would say, "My sister lifted up the claims of Christ to me when I was a young wife and mother, and He helped me see His holiness and my need of a Savior—He relieved me of my fears and changed my whole perspective of life."

19A. The Message paraphrases Proverbs 27:5 "A spoken reprimand is better than approval that's never expressed."

C. It is so easy to give advice quickly, off the top of one's head—but counsel of the soul prays, reflects, and seeks God before it speaks.

3. Love is a Choice

8B. These women were willing to make enormous sacrifices—leaving home, family, friends—even their own mothers. But when they realized it meant also being single, one turned back. It was very hard to be a woman without a man in those days. Orpah's choice is natural, but Ruth's was supernatural. There is symbolism here—when we come to a crossroads with Christ, most turn back – that is the natural response, for there is a cost.

4. But Ruth Clung to Her

19. This is an important question. The Christian life is a paradox, for it is in dying that we find life. How beautifully Ruth illustrates this, and Orpah, who clung to her old way of life, and then faded out of the pages of Scripture, illustrates the foolishness of that choice. Talk about what dying to self looks like for each of them.

5. Giving Our In-Laws Grace

15. Some feel Naomi went too far—only God knows. But surely James does caution us against being quick to be angry at God, and to be careful with our words, and to be willing to listen to Him. A similar warning is in Ecclesiastes 5:1–2. Yet God longs for our honesty too, for those who seemed to make Jesus the most angry were those who wanted to impress others with their piety, who might have acted "unruffled," but in truth, were just "whitewashed tombs full of dead men's bones." David's example in the psalms was to express his anxiety and his failures openly to God, even his despair at God seeming "silent," yet also, always come back to God's goodness.

6. The Romance in Ruth

12. STRUCTURING RUTH 2:1-2 (NKJV)

THERE WAS A RELATIVE

      OF NAOMI'S HUSBAND

      A MAN OF GREAT WEALTH

      OF THE FAMILY OF ELIMELECH

  HIS NAME WAS BOAZ

      SO

      RUTH

        THE MOABITESS

         SAID TO NAOMI

PLEASE LET ME GO TO THE FIELD

     AND

     GLEAN HEADS OF GRAIN

          AFTER HIM

           IN WHOSE SIGHT

            I MAY FIND FAVOR

Note the importance of the two independent phrases. Note the four things said about Boaz. Note the last two phrases and how they lead into the drama.

16. As soon as the harvesters pray a blessing on Boaz, he spots Ruth and inquires about her. He finds out there is no man in her life, but instead, a mother-in-law. Not only is she

available, she is going to be a great blessing to him as his future wife.

19. The identity of a woman was seen in connection to a father, husband, or sons. This helps us understand Naomi's desperation and the plight of both Naomi and Ruth.

7. *Matchmaker, Matchmaker*

8. When approaching someone with a request, it is so important to anticipate how they might feel. Naomi has thought about how to help Boaz "save face" if he chooses not to redeem Ruth, so she sends Ruth out quietly, under cover of night. She has Ruth put her best face forward, asking her to wash herself and to put on her best dress. Telling Ruth to uncover Boaz feet was a gentle and symbolic way, without being too direct, of asking Boaz to cover her with marriage. Naomi knew the cultural custom well enough that she was confident this would be clear to Boaz, and it was. It is important, when going to someone, that they understand exactly what you want to happen.

12C. Some may be surprised to discover through this passage that Esther actually slept with the king. So often we heard this story as children, the edited "Veggie Tales" version. They may be interested in studying *A Woman of Faith* for the whole story!

21. Be extremely sensitive on this subject of divorce. Often the church has failed miserably, being unwilling to permit divorce when God Himself has given permission in cases of adultery and abandonment. Perhaps we fear that if we condone it, even when the covenant has been broken, we weaken the fiber of marriage. But God warns against adding to what He has required. When we add to God's Word, we become cruel, and in this case, we add insult to injury. Though it is true that every individual is a sinner and fault can always be found in both parties, it is also true God recognizes "covenant-breakers" as having dealt treacherously with their spouses – and He has a heart of compassion for the victim – and so must we. This question might be a time to allow those who are divorced to share their feelings and their hope for how they will be treated by the church.

8. *Better Than Seven Sons*

10A. Boaz bought Elimelech's land, and he bought it from Naomi. She seems to continue to live on that land, with Boaz, Ruth, and her grandson, Obed. Boaz was certainly provider, protector, and a picture of our Redeemer.

14A. They built up the house of Israel – in other words, they were blessed with sons. Ruth had been barren, they were praying for fertility, and for sons.

16. Witnessing vows – for accountability. Prayer.

17. Many wedding traditions are based on that amazing day when Christ will come for His Bride, the body of true believers:

He longs for a pure and faithful bride, dressed in the pure white garment of salvation (Is. 1:18; Matt. 22:12); a salvation that is true so that it results in righteous acts (Rev. 19:7–8)

She will be adorned beautifully and He will be clothed in splendor and majesty (Ps.45) He will come with a trumpet sound (1 Thess. 4:16)

There will be a wedding banquet (Luke 14:15)

There will be many witnesses and a host of heaven rejoicing (Rev. 19:6)

23. Boaz and Ruth—Obed—Jesse—David—Jesus Christ

9. I Will Sing of My Redeemer

1. Symbolism in memory work:

Ruth 1:16–17

This is the kind of commitment God is looking for in us—to go where He asks us to go, to embrace His people, to make this a daily, lifelong commitment.

Ruth 2:10-13

To realize that despite our past, God has noticed us and shown us favor. He longs for us to leave our past and come under the shadow of His wings for refuge. We should pray for continued favor.

Ruth 3:9

Jesus is our Kinsman-Redeemer who covers us with His garment of righteousness, who takes us under His wing.

Ruth 4:15

Jesus will renew our life and sustain us, even in old age, for He is our Kinsman-Redeemer. We also, if we follow the model of Ruth, can be a great blessing of God to others.

Sources

1. Love in a Time of Famine

1. Larry Richards, *The Bible Reader's Companion* (Colorado Springs: Victor, 1991), 157.

2. Kenneth R. R. Gros Louis, *The Book of Judges* (Nashville: Abingdon, 1974), 147.

3. Dr. A. C. Hervey, "Judges," *The Pulpit Commentary*, vol. 3 (Peabody, MA: Hendrickson, n.d.), 194–95.

2. Distorted Love

1. Cyril J. Barber, *Ruth, an Expositional Commentary* (Chicago: Moody Press, 1983), 44.

2. Helmut Thielicke, *The Waiting Father* (New York: Harper, 1959), 24–26.

3. The International Standard Bible Encyclopedia, vol.3, "Moab" (Grand Rapids, Mich.: Eerdmans, 1986), 393.

3. Love is a Choice

1. Judith Kates, *Reading Ruth* (New York: Ballantine, 1990), 135.

2. Mike Mason, *The Gospel According to Job* (Wheaton, IL: Crossway, 1994), 153.

3. Ruth Anna Putnam, quoted in Kates, *Reading Ruth*, 45.

4. Gary Smalley and John Trent, *The Blessing* (New York: Pocket, 1986), 136–37.

5. Barber, Ruth, 55.

6. Charles Spurgeon, *Treasury of David II* (Peabody, MA: Hendrickson, n. d.), 88–89.

4. But Ruth Clung to Her

1. Murray D. Gowan, *The Book of Ruth* (Leicester, England: Apollos, 1992), 34.

2. Henry Moorhouse, *Ruth, the Moabitess, Gleanings from the Book of Ruth* (Chicago: The Bible Institute Colportage Association, 1881), 11.

3. Alicia Ostriker, quoted in Kates, *Reading Ruth*, 89.

4. Nehama Aschkenasy, quoted in ibid., 113.

5. Walter Trobisch, *I Married You* (New York: Harper, 1971), 18, 29.

6. J. Vernon McGee, *Ruth, the Romance of Redemption* (Nashville: Thomas Nelson, 1982), 62.

7. Avivah Zornberg, quoted in Kates, *Reading Ruth*, 66.

8. Jan Titterington, "Insights from the Book of Ruth," *His* (Jan. 1976): 8.

5. *Giving Our In-laws Grace*

1. Philip Yancey, *What's So Amazing About Grace?* (Grand Rapids, Mich.: Zondervan, 1997), 100.

2. David Atkinson, *The Message of Ruth* (Downers Grove, Ill.: InterVarsity, 1983), 10.

3. Gloria Golreich, quoted in Kates, *Reading Ruth*, 38.

4. Rabbi Ruth H. Sohn, quoted in ibid., 20.

5. Trobisch, *I Married You*, 17.

6. Merle Field, quoted in Kates, *Reading Ruth*, 174.

6. *The Romance in Ruth*

1. Samuel Cox, quoted in Barber, *Ruth*, p. 71.

2. G. Cambell Morgan, quoted in ibid., 33.

3. Robert A. Watson, quoted in McGee, *Ruth*, 78.

4. McGee, *Ruth*, 78.

5. Alexander Maclaren, quoted in David Atkinson, *The Message of Ruth: Wings of Refuge,* (Downers Grove, Ill.: InterVarsity, 1984), 64.

6. Barber, *Ruth*, 88.

7. Dr. Bob Schwartz, *Diets Don't Work!* (Las Vegas, NV: Breakthru Publishing , 1982), 80.

7. *Matchmaker, Matchmaker*

1. McGee, *Ruth*, 88, 93.

2. Barber, *Ruth*, 101.

8. *Better than Seven Sons!*

1. Atkinson, *The Message of Ruth*, 116.

9. *I Will Sing of My Redeemer*

1. McGee, *Ruth*, 138.

2. Yancey, *What's So Amazing About Grace*, 54.

3. P. Trible, quoted in Frederic W. Bush, ed., et. al., *Word Biblical Commentary*, vol. 9 "Ruth-Esther" (Nashville: Nelson, 1996), 54.

DEE BRESTIN MAKES GOD'S WORD CLEAR TO WOMEN . . .

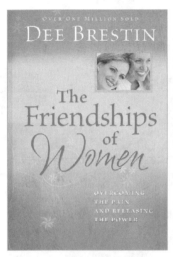

The Friendships of Women

Thousands of women have read this book and have been transformed in their thinking on friendships. In this classic bestseller, Dee Brestin examines the biblical friendship of Ruth and Naomi that reveals a pattern for friendship that will help women discover and focus their gift for intimacy.

ISBN-13: 978-0-78144-316-6 • ISBN-10: 0-78144-316-4
Item #: 104038 • Paperback • $10.99

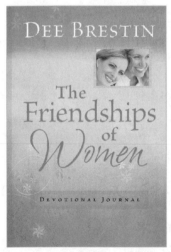

The Friendships of Women Devotional Journal

Now there's a devotional journal to help readers record their thoughts and meditations after each chapter. Each chapter starts with a scripture verse, a message point, a reflective question and text. Women are prompted to write their ideas in the lines provided in this attractive journal, for a more meaningful and lasting application of God's word.

ISBN-13: 978-1-56292-725-7 • ISBN-10: 1-56292-725-6
Item #: 104572 • Hardcover • $12.99

...AND TOUCHES THEIR HEARTS THROUGH MEANINGFUL WORDS.

A Woman of Hospitality

This eight-chapter study guides women in practicing the biblical command to be hospitable. It also includes a special section on hospitality and the holidays.

ISBN-13: 978-0-78144-333-3 • ISBN-10: 0-78144-333-4
Item #: 104582 • 128 Pages • Paperback • $9.99

A Woman of Wisdom

Based on Proverbs, this book explores ten characteristics of honorable character, including awe of God, discretion, trust, faithfulness, and honesty.

ISBN-13: 978-0-78144-332-6 • ISBN-10: 0-78144-332-6
Item #: 104581 • 128 Pages • Paperback • $9.99

A Woman of Purpose

Many believe the key sources for Luke were the women who traveled with Jesus, which explains why the Book of Luke so warms the hearts of women. This study looks at 12 issues that are particularly intriguing to women.

ISBN-13: 978-0-78144-334-0 • ISBN-10: 0-78144-334-2
Item #: 104583 • 128 Pages • Paperback • $9.99

A Woman of Worship

An in depth study on some of our most beautiful psalms accompanied by audio CD from Integrity Music that ties thematically to each chapter. Some of the chapter headings include: Shout to the Lord, Whiter Than Snow, Give Thanks.

ISBN-13: 978-0-78144-335-7 • ISBN-10: 0-78144-335-0
Item #: 104584 • 128 Pages • Paperback • $12.99

To order, visit www.cookministries.com,
call 1-800-323-7543, or visit your favorite local bookstore.